M000298406

Santa Fe
Railway

Brian Solomon

MBI

To Brian L. Jennison—
A fan of the Santa Fe

First published in 2003 by Motorbooks International, Galtier Plaza, Suite 200, 380 Jackson Street, St. Paul, MN 55101-3885 USA

Motorbooks International titles are also available at discounts in bulk quantity for industrial or sales-promotional use. For details write to Special Sales Manager at Motorbooks International Wholesalers & Distributors, Galtier Plaza, Suite 200, 380 Jackson Street, St. Paul, MN 55101-3885 USA

ISBN 0-7603-1072-6

On the front cover:
Santa Fe 914 was designated by the railroad as a DASH 8-41CW, this later General Electric DASH 8 model (Santa Fe nos. 867 to 951) featured an improved radiator design known as Split Cooling. As a result these locomotives had a slightly higher rating of 4,135 hp, rather than 4,000 hp of the 800 to 866 series that were designated DASH 8-40CW. This designation difference was made by the railroad, rather than the manufacturer.

On the frontispiece:
Santa Fe 250 was brand new when photographed on September 5, 1995. Although the railroad name would disappear into the corporate wash of BNSF, the Warbonnet livery survived a little longer as several subsequent orders of BNSF locomotives were delivered in Warbonnet paint.

On the title page:
In 1989, Santa Fe reintroduced its famous Warbonnet livery, much to the delight of railroad enthusiasts and photographers. The colorful combination of silver, red, and yellow is was one of Santa Fe's most distinctive attributes in the diesel era.

On the back cover:
Some of the finest steam powered locomotives ever built were Santa Fe's late-era Northerns. Its 2900 class, built during World War II, were massive, but fast machines. They weighed more than a half-million pounds, making them the very heaviest 4-8-4s, and were capable of speeds of 100 mph in regular service. The class leader, 2900, is seen racing across the New Mexico desert in the mid 1940s with a 12 car passenger train in tow.

Edited by Peter Schletty
Designed by Design53, St. Paul, Minnesota

Printed in China

Contents

Acknowledgments

I have many good memories of the Santa Fe railroad and the people I've experienced it with. It would not have been possible to write this book without their help, and the help of many others. I would especially like to thank my father, Richard Jay Solomon, for introducing me to the Santa Fe and for the generous use of his photographs, timetables, and books. Thanks also to Tim Doherty for the use of his library. Several photographers have contributed photographs to this project; they are credited by each image, and their contributions are very much appreciated. Special thanks to Dave and Helen Burton, not just for photos, but for providing me with lodging and entertainment at Tehachapi. Don Marson, a onetime employee of the Santa Fe, was generous with his photographs and very helpful in my understanding of the Santa Fe's latter-day operations. Special thanks to Don and his wife, Linnay, for Christmas dinner 1995, when Don was working at Santa Fe's offices in Schaumburg, Illinois. Tom Kline provided many excellent photos of Santa Fe operations in Texas, Oklahoma, and New Mexico. He also assisted in captioning, a task for which I am especially grateful. Robert A. Buck of Tucker's Hobbies in Warren, Massachusetts, encouraged my interest in the Santa Fe, and recalled for me his own trip on Santa Fe's *Grand Canyon*. Mike and Tom Danneman and I took several trips to photograph Santa Fe operations in Illinois, and Mike provided some excellent photos for this book, as did Illinois-based photographer Steve Smedley. Coy at the Denver Public Library helped me with the acquisition of historical images, as did J. R. Quinn. Mike Blaszak, whom I came to know working at *Pacific RailNews*, assisted my understanding of the modern Santa Fe and its role as an intermodal giant. Lastly, thanks to everyone who worked for the railroad and who made it great.

Cadiz, California, is a desert oasis along Santa Fe's Needles District in the Mojave Desert. Santa Fe's line to Parker and Phoenix joined the mainline here. It was the location of both fuel and water storage, vital necessities in a desert where both commodities are scarce. *Photo by Brian Solomon*

Introduction

The Santa Fe Railway's charisma and mystique have long made it one of America's compelling railways. It blends our nation's westward vision and the appeal of the Southwest with all the best elements of railroading: colorful, sexy passenger trains, attractive stations, fascinating historical personalities, a diverse and eclectic collection of locomotives and, of course, lots of long freight trains.

The popularity of the Santa Fe is a tribute to great public relations and successful advertising. From its earliest days Santa Fe promoted western travel and incorporated traditional Southwestern motifs in its advertising literature. Its later day heralds and paint liveries drew strongly from these ancient symbols. Certainly the Santa Fe is one of the best known of all railways, and its striking red, yellow, black, and silver "Warbonnet" livery,

Above: Rolling eastbound, a Santa Fe intermodal train climbs at Sand Cut, California, on March 28, 1992. The late-era Santa Fe blended some of the best elements of traditional and modern railroading. *Photo by Brian Solomon*

Left: Santa Fe's corporate image thrived on the compelling mystique of the American Southwest incorporating Native American styles and motifs in its logos and symbols. Fred Matthews captured Santa Fe's logo on the side of an Electro-Motive F unit. *Photo by Fred Matthews*

which mimics Native American headdress, is the most recognizable railroad paint scheme.

My personal acquaintance with the Santa Fe began when a pair of O-Scale Warbonnet Lionel F3s made their debut in our house Christmas morning 1972. That event 30 years ago still sticks in my mind. I wonder how many other children had similar experiences. My father still has his 1948 Lionel catalog that prompted this belated locomotive acqui-

Top: Toluca, Illinois, is one of many small towns served by the Santa Fe mainline from Chicago to Los Angeles. *Photo by Brian Solomon*

Below: At twilight on March 25, 1995, an eastbound Santa Fe train races through Toluca, Illinois, on its way to Chicago. *Photo by Brian Solomon*

sition. As a child growing up in New England I was fascinated by railroading in the Mojave Desert, a place I could only imagine.

In 1980, I finally saw the Santa Fe for the first time on a family holiday to California and took a ride on a former Santa Fe dome operating on Amtrak's *Coast Starlight* over Southern Pacific rails from Oakland to Los Angeles. This visit inspired my migration to California in 1989 after graduating from college. During my five years living in the Golden State I explored Franklin Canyon, the San Joaquin Valley, Santa Fe's operations over SP's line through the Tehachapis. I visited the legendary Santa Fe places such as Cajon Pass, Barstow, and the Needles District across the Mojave. Later, I made trips to Arizona, New Mexico, and Kansas (albeit briefly), as well as Illinois, to look at Santa Fe's lines and operations. Many of my California excursions were made with friends and fellow photographers, including T. S. Hoover, J. D. Schmid, and Brian L. Jennison, a fellow enthusiast and railway photographer, some of whose images appear in this book. Of the Santa Fe, Brian wrote in *Pacific RailNews'* November 1995 tribute to the Santa Fe, ". . . in the railfan world, nobody doesn't like Santa Fe. Even if it isn't your absolute favorite big Western railroad, it's almost certainly a close second." He goes on to ask, "What's not to like?"

I left California in 1994 for Wisconsin, where I worked on various Pentrex magazines, including *Pacific RailNews* (PRN), which I edited during one of the most tumultuous periods in modern American railroad history. During a little more than two years, some of the oldest and best-known names in railroading vanished in a fury pace of corporate merger and consolidation. In June 1994, a month before I started at PRN, Santa Fe and

Burlington Northern announced their merger. A few months later, Union Pacific put in a competing bid for Santa Fe, which resulted in a flurry of competing press releases, editorials, and news. Burlington Northern ultimately prevailed over UP as Santa Fe's suitor. Then UP turned to gobble up two other traditional western carriers—first acquiring its longtime partner in transcontinental traffic, Chicago & North Western, and a year later conquering the great Southern Pacific, that western railroad with which Santa Fe had tried to merge just a decade earlier. Mega Merger Mania, as we called it, would continue for a few more years, and more lines would disappear.

One of the highlights of working for *Pacific RailNews* was when Art Director and Managing Editor Tom Danneman and I arranged with the Santa Fe to photograph its very last new locomotive. Thanks to the help of our correspondent Mike Blaszak, Santa Fe's public relations representative, Mike Martin, and Santa Fe's shop crews at Corwith, on September 5, 1995, Tom and I were able to pose Santa Fe SD75M No. 250 for the cover of the magazine. We knew that the end of the Santa Fe as a distinctive and independent railway was only a few weeks away. There would never be another new Santa Fe locomotive. We also wondered what would become of the dearly loved Warbonnet livery. Would this be the last new locomotive so painted? (As it turned out, BNSF adopted the Warbonnet for a short time and more locomotives were delivered in red and silver, albeit lettered BNSF instead of Santa Fe.) A generation earlier my father had witnessed the end of another era, as he had traveled on the last of the great passenger trains, including Santa Fe's own *Super Chief*. Now, I was seeing some of America's best-known railroads disappear.

Looking west on the Needles District near old Trojan in California's Mojave Desert: the silhouette of well-polished rails at sunset will remain an image of the Santa Fe. *Photo by Brian Solomon*

While the old Santa Fe comprises an important component to BNSF, and much of its corporate symbolism has been incorporated by BNSF, the new company does not have the compelling draw that Santa Fe had. Sure, BNSF runs many long freight trains and yes, as of this writing in 2002, the odd Warbonnet painted locomotive survives. But BNSF is not the railroad founded by Cyrus K. Holliday, and it was not the line responsible for the famous *Chiefs*, and does not have the mystique and popular appeal of the Santa Fe. As I write this in Dublin, Ireland, the Santa Fe has been gone from the scene the better part of seven years. Has it really been that long? I find it hard to believe that there aren't five clean new Warbonnets racing toward California with the 199 in tow. The tracks are there, but the flare and continuity are gone. The Santa Fe may be gone, but its spirit lives on. This book is a collection of Santa Fe images designed to portray the spirit of the Santa Fe Railway. Please enjoy!

Chapter 1

Santa Fe History

Perhaps no other railroad's geographical names remind one of its past better than Santa Fe's. To travel over its rails, or inspect its line, one is reminded of the history that made the railroad great. Barstow, Kingman, Seligman, and Holbrook are strategic stations on Santa Fe's transcontinental mainline, and all named for important men in Santa Fe's early history. The modest burg of Holliday, Kansas, although not a particularly important place on the railroad, is a good place to start the story of the Santa Fe. It was named for Cyrus Kurtz Holliday, the visionary behind the railroad that became known as Santa Fe, and one of the railroad's greatest proponents in its formative years. Cyrus K. Holliday, born in 1826, was one of the founders of Topeka, Kansas. In 1857, Holliday helped conceive a railroad plan to connect nearby Atchison with Topeka. In 1860, he helped found the Atchison & Topeka Railroad. It would be a few years yet before any track would be laid, and Atchison would not be the first destination.

In those pioneering days, the Santa Fe Trail was an established route west. The trail became especially popular following the California Gold Rush, when thousands of fortune seekers worked their way west over this route. The Santa Fe Trail was not a specific road, but rather a network of paths across the western plains and deserts. To those in the East, the Santa Fe Trail conveyed the spirit and mystique of the American Southwest. In 1863, when Holliday's railroad changed its

Crisp dessert sun shines on the fresh paint of a brand new Santa Fe General Electric diesel. *Photo by Brian Solomon*

Kansas was the birthplace of the Santa Fe, eventually reaching from the West Coast to Chicago. On the evening of January 8, 1994, a Santa Fe eastbound led by a GP20 roars through Lebo, Kansas. *Photo by Don Marson*

Topeka was often viewed as "The home of the Santa Fe." This Kansas city is the State capital, and was the location of the Santa Fe general offices, a company hospital, and important shops and yards. This view depicts the shops as they appeared in the late nineteenth century, although the card was posted in 1907. By the 1940s, the Topeka shops occupied 293 acres. *Postcard from author's collection*

Santa Fe R. R. Shops.   Topeka, Kans.

I'm having a grand time in Topeka.
Does this look natural? *Kate.*

The Hall Stationery Co., Distr., Topeka, Kans. June 26, 1907.

name to the Atchison, Topeka & Santa Fe (AT&SF), he hoped to capitalize on the romantic intrigue of the great American West. At that time, the trading settlement of Santa Fe (established in 1598) was a goal beyond the horizon. It represented a romantic ideal. By adding it to the name of the railroad, Holliday was in effect calling the railroad the "Here, There & Far West." "Santa Fe" filled the space at the end of the name, occupied by "Pacific" in many other roads of the time. As it happened, Santa Fe remained a purely conceptual destination for some years. The Civil War and lack of finances delayed Holliday's line.

Finally, in 1868, with help from Congress, the Santa Fe began construction. Santa Fe operated its first train in 1869, and by 1872 had built a line clear across Kansas to the Colorado border in order to fulfill the obligations of a substantial land grant. In the 1860s, and 1870s, the United States government gave out generous land grants to private companies

as an incentive to build railroads westward. A great difficulty in building western lines was building across enormous distances without significant sources of on-line revenue. It was one thing to build a railroad between established cities in the East, where passenger and freight revenue could be assured from the very beginning with each new town reached, but such was the case in the West.

This is the legacy of the Santa Fe: it not only built a railway, but effectively developed the communities along its lines; thus the many towns along the way named in honor of Santa Fe builders and officials. The Santa Fe finally reached Atchison in 1872. Interestingly enough, none of the railroad's namesakes—Atchison, Topeka, or Santa Fe—were situated on the railroad's later transcontinental route, although Topeka was an important shop town and housed the railroad's general offices for many years.

In the 1870s, Santa Fe initiated multifaceted advertising campaigns promoting not just its lines, but the territory it served. A brochure called "The San Juan Guide" encouraged settlement and tourism in Colorado. The early days of the Santa Fe were synonymous with the halcyon days of the Wild West, an era of cowboys, immigrant settlers, and lawless characters. The advent of barbed wire in the early 1870s combined with the practical, and comparatively inexpensive, transportation offered by Santa Fe and other railroads permitted the rapid settlement and cultivation of the Kansas and Oklahoma plains. Open-range cattle farming and wheat fields took the place of the buffalo range. The Santa Fe doomed the great buffalo herds and the way of life enjoyed by Native Americans who had coexisted with these animals for centuries, and it profited from the transport of settlers and the agricultural produce they harvested.

One of the most colorful episodes of Santa Fe's westward expansion was the railroad's territorial posturing with General William Jackson Palmer's Denver & Rio Grande (DRG). In 1878, both lines vied for control of the vital Raton Pass in the mountains on the border with Colorado and New Mexico, and both sent in construction parties. Santa Fe prevailed here with the help of Richens L. Wootton, better known as "Uncle Dick" Wootton, a Virginia-born pioneer who operated the toll road over Raton. Santa Fe and Rio Grande fought later, quite literally, with scouts, spies, mercenaries, and guns for control of the Royal Gorge of the Arkansas, a narrow cleft in the mountains needed to reach booming mining districts in southwestern Colorado. A complex series of events saw several people shot, and briefly resulted in Santa

A World War I vintage postcard view of Santa Fe's general offices in Topeka, Kansas. The name Topeka loosely translated means "a grand place to dig potatoes." *Postcard from author's collection*

Seligman, Arizona, like many locations along the Santa Fe, was named for one of the railroad's early builders: C. E. Seligman. The town became a strategic point for the company, serving as a division point and the location of a moderate-sized yard. By the 1990s, Seligman's heyday as a railroad hub had come and gone. On July 13, 1990, a westbound is seen passing the station. *Photo by George S. Pitarys*

Fe leasing Palmer's DRG, only to later relinquish control. Ultimately, peace was made and Rio Grande secured its hold on the Colorado mine traffic while forcing Santa Fe to focus its sights westward.

By this time the Santa Fe was under the direction of William Barstow Strong, for whom the important California location is named. Strong, who was elevated to president of the line in 1881, pushed Santa Fe expansion at a furious pace. In 1880, the Santa Fe railroad reached Albuquerque, New Mexico. It chose to avoid the city of Santa Fe because of the geographical and operational hardship it would have caused. (Instead, the railroad's namesake was reached by an 18-mile branch off the mainline running from Lamy.)

That year, Santa Fe and the St. Louis & San Francisco (a line later known as the "Frisco") arranged to jointly build the Atlantic & Pacific, a railroad designed by charter to connect Tulsa and California. Lewis Kingman was the engineer who located the A&P routing, while H. R. Holbrook was the chief engineer for the line. Both men were honored with towns named for them created along the lines in Arizona, as were General Edward N. Winslow, president of the St.L&SF, and C. E. Seligman, an A&P construction engineer.

Simultaneously, with its westward push Santa Fe arranged with the Mexican government to build a line to a Pacific port at Guaymas, Mexico. In the process of reaching Mexico, Santa Fe connected with the Southern Pacific at

Deming, New Mexico, thus technically forming America's second transcontinental railroad link (the first was established at Promontory Point, Utah, on May 10, 1869, when Central Pacific joined rails with Union Pacific). Southern Pacific, the dominent western carrier, wasn't keen on moving traffic through this gateway, and so the Deming route never amounted to much. After reaching the California border at Needles in 1883, Santa Fe received a similar level of cooperation from SP, which had built a line across the Mojave Desert to meet the A&P. Strong overcame this initial difficulty with SP, and ultimately Santa Fe assumed control of this crucial line to California. In 1885, Santa Fe finished its route over California's Cajon Pass, reaching the Pacific port of San Diego by way of an inland line through Temecula Canyon. This route proved unsatisfactory when flash floods destroyed the right-of-way

Santa Fe operated a branch in the Bay Area from its yards at Richmond to Oakland, California, in the very heart of Southern Pacific's operations. On March 23, 1979, a local freight is seen departing Emeryville for Richmond passing a traditional "wig wag" grade crossing signal. Notice the Santa Fe 'Chief' herald on the building to the right. This old warehouse was, at the time, home to the East Bay Society of Model Engineers. *Photo by Brian Jennison*

On the clear winter morning of January 23, 1991, a Santa Fe westbound climbs Ash Hill through the barren Mojave landscape between Siberia and Klondike, California. The east- and west-bound tracks are on different alignments on this portion of the Ash Hill grade, and the eastward track can be seen in the distance. *Photo by Brian Solomon*

in the canyon, but by 1887 Santa Fe had reached Los Angeles, and in 1888, Santa Fe completed a better route to San Diego.

While Santa Fe was securing its position in southern California, it simultaneously was arranging routes into Texas. In May 1886, the Atchison, Topeka & Santa Fe acquired a line called the Gulf Coast & Santa Fe (GC&SF), a line over which, despite the similarity in name, the AT&SF had no previous influence. Over the previous decade the GC&SF had constructed lines north from the post of Galveston. Following AT&SF control, the GC&SF built northward to meet an AT&SF line building south in order to link the two systems. As a result of Texas legislation requiring railroads operating within the state to be headquartered locally, the Gulf Coast & Santa Fe survived as a Santa Fe subsidiary. In addition to its main routes, Santa Fe also built up a myriad of branchlines in Kansas, Oklahoma, and southern California.

A Santa Fe local works Port Chicago on the line from Stockton to Richmond, California, on August 15, 1975. Port Chicago was named in honor of Santa Fe's eastern terminus. The west end of Santa Fe's system in Northern California was largely operated as single track with semaphore block signals. In later years the semaphores were replaced by Union Switch & Signal searchlights, common on much of the Santa Fe. *Photo by Brian Jennison*

Santa Fe became increasingly dissatisfied with its eastward connections from Kansas City, and in 1887 decided to build its own line to Chicago, despite the fact that several other railways already connected to the two major hubs. Wasting no time, Santa Fe built an "airline" route between Kansas City and Chicago, incorporating a portion of the Chicago & St. Louis line, between Chicago and Ancona, Illinois. Service to Chicago began in 1888, and this new line gave Santa Fe the only through route from Chicago to California under the control of one company. By contrast, the "Overland Route" was jointly operated by Chicago & North Western, Union Pacific, and Southern Pacific's Central Pacific. Santa Fe's line remained the only such through route to California for many years.

Of the characters associated with the Santa Fe at this time, perhaps none was more colorful than British-born Fred Harvey. Harvey emigrated to America in the 1850s and made his way west, where he worked in a variety of jobs before becoming a western freight agent for Burlington. At that time, railroads typically off-loaded passengers at strategic locations for rushed meals at dodgy railroad "beaneries." This experience was generally unpleasant and considered one of the great detractions to long-distance railway travel. Harvey felt he could improve upon this experience and proposed the introduction of quality railroad eateries on the Burlington. But, Burlington foolishly dismissed the idea, and in 1876 Harvey approached Charles F. Morse of the Santa Fe (and a former Burlington employee), who accepted his offer.

His first restaurant for the Santa Fe was located at Topeka. He was extremely successful

Barstow's Harvey House station and restaurant lies to the east of Santa Fe's enormous yards and locomotive shop. This handsome building was the work of Francis W. Wilson. Like other Santa Fe stations, such as those in Needles and San Diego, the Barstow station exhibits a Spanish-Moor style that was popular in the region. An eastbound train passes the famous building as it begins its trip across the Needles District. *Photo by Brian Solomon*

Many locations along Santa Fe's Needles District were named for bleak or desolate-sounding places, and so Bagdad, California, reminds one of its more famous counterpart in present-day Iraq. In steam days all trains would have stopped here for water. Since only salt water could be obtained at Bagdad, every day Santa Fe brought in roughly 20 cars of water from Newberry Springs, located about 56 miles to the west. *Photo by Brian Solomon*

in this enterprise and soon he was operating many restaurants along the Santa Fe (while maintaining his employment at the Burlington). Harvey's high culinary standards, and attractive and unmarried waitresses (popularly known as "Harvey Girls"), helped make his restaurants very popular with travelers. Over time he expanded his business to include hotels, and later he also operated Santa Fe's dining cars. Today the Harvey story is part of the Santa Fe legend.

At the end of the 1880s, Santa Fe's finances began to stall as a result of its intensive expansion and Strong resigned his presidency. As the 1890s dawned, the railroad entered a tumultuous period that saw it acquire the St. Louis & San Francisco and Colorado Midland lines. Following the great financial panic of 1893, the company underwent a dramatic reorganization, from which it emerged without the two recent acquisitions, and renamed itself the Santa Fe Railway. At this time, the dynamic Ed Ripley took the helm of the Santa Fe and over the next two decades implemented many improvements to the railway while the line enjoyed an enormous growth in traffic.

Pass, SP was convinced instead to acquiesce trackage rights between Mojave and Bakersfield. With these two railroads using the line, the twisting Tehachapi crossing grew to become one of the biggest bottlenecks in western railroad operations (and certainly one the favorite places to observe railroad operations, as well as spectacular scenery, twisting looping trackage, and constant heavy railroad

Santa Fe's Mazon depot was located 66 miles west of Chicago on the line's raceway from Chicago to Kansas City. Most of Santa Fe's big-named passenger trains, the *Super Chief, Chief, El Capitan,* and the like, raced on past tiny Mazon, yet train numbers 123 and 124, the *Grand Canyon,* would stop here for the benefit of long-distance passengers. *Photo by Steve Smedley*

Once a very popular crossing protection device, the "wig-wag" signal alerted motorists by it's swinging "banjo" and red light. These simple electromechanical devices were phased out by modern electronically operated signals on many railroads, but remained in use on the Santa Fe in numerous locations until the mid-1990s. On January 5, 1985, a wig-wag protects the passage of a northbound freight just east of Bellville, Texas, on the Galveston Subdivision. *Photo by Tom Kline*

During the mid-1890s, Santa Fe encouraged the construction of the San Francisco & San Joaquin Valley Railroad through its namesake valley located in the heart of SP's infamous transportation monopoly. To reach the SF&SJ, Santa Fe needed to get across the difficult terrain in the Tehachapis, where SP's mainline had run since 1876. While Santa Fe considered building a line of equal sinuosity to SP's tortuous crossing by way of the nearby Tejon

At sunrise on September 23, 1998—three years and a day after the Burlington Northern Santa Fe merger—an eastbound waits for a signal near Sais, New Mexico. Although the Santa Fe has vanished into the BNSF, its lines remain extremely busy, and freight traffic has continued to grow. Following the merger, BNSF set out to increase capacity of former Santa Fe lines by adding many miles of double-track Centralized Traffic Control to routes formerly restricted by the limits of single-track CTC operation. *Photo by Brian Solomon*

activity). At this time Santa Fe also undertook additional expansion in the Texas Panhandle region, completed under the guise of its Panhandle & Santa Fe subsidiary.

The Twentieth-Century Santa Fe

In the decade after the turn of the century, Santa Fe joined with SP in the incorporation of the Northwestern Pacific, a line running from the Bay Area up through the redwood forests and along the Eel River Canyon to Eureka. Southern Pacific and Santa Fe each owned half the NWP until Santa Fe sold out to SP in the 1920s.

One of the most important lines in Santa Fe's latter-day operations was the so-called Belen Cutoff completed in 1908 to connect its east–west mainline at Dalies, (west of Albuquerque) with its Texas Panhandle lines at Texico by way of Clovis, New Mexico and over the summit at Mountainair. By linking the Belen Cutoff with other lines (which were upgraded for heavier traffic), Santa Fe developed an alternative southerly transcontinental route to its original line that ran via Albuquerque, New Mexico, and La Junta, Colorado. The Belen Cutoff faced much easier grades than its older line, which crossed the difficult Glorieta and Raton mountain passes. As its transcontinental freight traffic developed, Santa Fe tended to route much of it via the Belen Cutoff, while sending most of its famous passenger trains over the northerly line via Raton.

The most difficult section of the Belen Cutoff is the eastbound grade from Belen to Mountainair through Abo Canyon. This was a helper district in steam days, and the location of one of Santa Fe's first Centralized Traffic Control (CTC) installations during World War II. CTC signaling increased line capacity by giving a remote operator control of both switches and signals, and allowing trains to proceed strictly by signal indication.

Another important link in Santa Fe's network was the Coleman Cutoff, completed in 1914. This new route by way of Coleman, Texas, linked Santa Fe's lines in central Texas more directly with the new Belen Cutoff transcontinental route to California, allowing Santa Fe to compete more effectively with SP's Sunset Route. The Coleman Cutoff shortened the distance of Santa Fe's route between Galveston and California by roughly 475 miles. Incidentally, Coleman, Texas, was named for Robert M. Coleman, a Lone Star

On the rocky ledge above Abo Canyon, the ground below trembles as the head end of an eastbound freight grinds its way up the 1.25 percent grade and across Bridge No. 7 on September 25, 1995. Marking the eastern end of the narrow canyon, Bridge No. 7 spans the dry Abo River Wash, which the railroad crosses seven times as it snakes it's way through this short three-mile canyon in the Manzanno Mountain range, 26 miles east of Belen. *Photo by Tom Kline*

pioneer, who should not be confused with Santa Fe's Richard Coleman, a surveyor and builder of the railroad's western lines.

In 1928, Santa Fe bought the American portion of the Kansas City, Mexico & Orient Railway, a line that ran diagonally across Kansas, Oklahoma, and Texas, reaching the Mexican border crossing at Presidio, Texas. Santa Fe continued to build and acquire new lines until the onset of the Great Depression. The railroad reached its peak in 1931, when it had 13,568 miles. At that time, Santa Fe was the longest railroad in the United States, a title it held until the big mergers of the 1960s. During the 1930s, the shrinking of the economy and "dust bowl" conditions resulted in

some branch line abandonment. Further retrenchment occurred during World War II, when scrap-iron drives encouraged the lifting of lightly used lines.

In the postwar era, Santa Fe evolved as a progressive modern railroad, investing in many new streamlined passenger trains, and upgrading its freight facilities. Santa Fe substantially rebuilt its most important yards. In 1949, its new electrically controlled hump yard at Argentine, Kansas (near Kansas City), opened replacing a traditional flat switching facility. Kansas City was one of Santa Fe's most important interchange points, where it connected with 12 other railroads. At Chicago, Santa Fe's eastern ter-

Santa Fe operated an extensive branch line network in Kansas, Oklahoma, and Texas, which served the agricultural communities it helped develop in the latter part of the 19th and early 20th centuries. This lightly used branch near Pratt, Kansas, was typical of those lines. *Photo by Brian Solomon*

minus and its other major interchange, the railroad also modernized its facilities and opened a state-of-the-art 32-track hump in 1958. The advent of dieselization changed the way the railroad operated freight trains. Diesels permitted Santa Fe to run much heavier and longer trains, and made starting such trains easier. Yard tracks were lengthened to accommodate longer freight consists and to minimize the time required in assembling trains ready to head out on the road. Diesels also eliminated the need for helpers in many locations.

Santa Fe was one of just a few railroads to implement major new construction after World War II. It improved its Dallas access in 1955 with the completion of a 48-mile cutoff. Then, in the late 1950s and early 1960s, it undertook two substantial line relocations in Arizona, both aimed at reducing grades and curvature to improve transit times and lower operating costs. These were the 44-mile Crookton line relocations between Crookton and Williams, opened to traffic in December 1960, and the Abra–Scull Valley line relocation on Santa Fe's "Peavine" route to Phoenix, which opened in April 1960.

Also in the 1960s, new branches were built to secure new traffic, such as the line to York Canyon in New Mexico (see chapter 3). Line and plant improvements continued into the 1970s. The lowering of the Cajon Summit crossing by 50 feet in 1972 was completed in conjunction with the introduction of CTC operations on this very busy mountain crossing. In addition to Santa Fe's traffic between the L.A. Basin and San Diego, Cajon also handled Union Pacific traffic moving over the Los Angeles & Salt Lake Route, which used trackage rights over the Santa Fe to reach the L.A. Basin.

This one-of-a-kind depot at Shawnee, Oklahoma, is unlikely to be confused with any other on Santa Fe lines. It was built in 1903, when the railroad pushed its way south through the state. It embodies a mix of architectural styles and is patterned after Romanesque and Gothic designs. The station's builder, Joseph Schuettner, from Aurora, Illinois, intended it as a clock tower, but clocks were never installed and instead heralds were placed over the clock positions. The station, which is located alongside the Shawnee Branch, now houses a museum containing railroad memorabilia and items of local history. The depot was constructed alongside what was once the freight mainline through Oklahoma. The Santa Fe built two north-south mainlines through the state paralleling each other but separated by a distance of 30 to 40 miles. The passenger main ran from Arkansas City, Kansas straight down through Oklahoma City and on to Gainesville, Texas. The freight main, which was built later, branched east off the passenger line at Newkirk, Oklahoma, and turned south down through the towns of Fairfax, Cushing, and Shawnee, before rejoining the passenger main at Pauls Valley. This arrangement separated freight and passenger operations in Oklahoma City and kept the railroad fluid during times of heavy traffic. As operating costs rose, freight traffic reverted back to the passenger main, while the freight line was partially abandoned in segments, with the remains surviving today as branchlines.

Text and Photo by Tom Kline

An eastbound crosses the Colorado River at Topock. This bridge opened in March 1945, to replace an earlier structure. From here, the train will begin the long climb to the summit at Flagstaff, Arizona. The first portion of this ascent is the 114-mile climb to a summit near Yampai, which is often credited as the longest unbroken main line grade in the United States. *Photo by Brian Solomon*

The Toledo, Peoria & Western was a Midwestern line that provided Santa Fe with an interchange shortcut that avoided Chicago. In 1960, Santa Fe and Pennsylvania divided control of the TP&W. Following the Conrail merger in 1976, Santa Fe became the sole owner of the TP&W, and merged the line into its system in 1984. During the 1960s, Santa Fe explored mergers with other lines, and seriously proposed buying the Western Pacific, but the merger was denied by the Interstate Commerce Commission (ICC) in 1965. That same year, Santa Fe officially merged its two Texas subsidiaries. In 1967, Santa Fe underwent a significant corporate restructuring that saw the creation of a holding company called Santa Fe Industries. During the 1980s, western railroad mergers were the order of the day. Burlington Northern absorbed the St. Louis & San Francisco, while Union Pacific, Missouri Pacific, and Western Pacific combined to form a much bigger and more powerful Union Pacific system.

In order to match its competition, Santa Fe looked to merge with rival Southern Pacific (SP), first proposing the combination in 1980, and again more seriously in 1983. At the end of that year, the two companies merged their holding companies to create Santa Fe Southern Pacific (SPSF), while

Moving slowly across the single-track drawbridge, DASH 8-40CW 809 crosses from the mainland to Galveston Island with a potash drag bound for the city's docks for export. In the background the lights of the many refineries that rim the bay in Texas City are visible in the twilight on this August 24, 1996, evening. The original bridge at this location, replaced in 1988, was built in the early 1910s and was as wide as the causeway, carrying the Santa Fe's rails, a interurban track, and a two-lane roadway over Galveston Bay. *Photo by Tom Kline*

anticipating ICC approval of the railroad merger. Confident of the ICC's positive decision, both railroads adopted a new paint livery that used SP red and Santa Fe yellow, which was applied to many locomotives on both lines. To the great surprise of both railroads and the entire railroad industry, the ICC declared the SPSF merger anticompetitive and rejected it in July 1986. This episode was a defining junction in Santa Fe's future.

Following the failed merger with Santa Fe, the company underwent changes in leadership, resulting in Robert Krebs taking control. The dynamic and resourceful Krebs had come to Santa Fe by way of the SP, and led the railroad in its final years. Following the SP debacle, Santa Fe shed many of its various branches and secondary lines, selling them to short-line operators and state agencies. The trimmed-down Santa Fe was preening itself for another merger attempt. At the end of June 1994, Santa Fe and Burlington North-ern announced their intent to merge. This precipitated a counteroffer for Santa Fe from Union Pacific.

Ultimately, the BN-SF combination prevailed. The ICC approved the BN-SF merger in July 1995, and the two holding companies merged on September 22 of that year. Railroad operations were coordinated several months later. Former Santa Fe routes and traffic remained an integral component of today's BNSF, which is one of America's four largest railways.

In the summer of 1993, weeks of extreme Midwestern weather resulted in terrible flooding along the region's river valleys that severely disrupted railroad operations. Santa Fe was among the hardest hit. Some of the worst flooding occurred at Fort Madison, Iowa, where the Santa Fe crossed the Mississippi River. The Fort Madison station is seen in August 1993 deluged by the over flowing waters of the Mississippi. *Photo by Steve Smedley.*

In anticipation of the Santa Fe and Southern Pacific railroad merger, the two companies adopted a new paint scheme that incorporated the colors of both railroads. Its colorful scarlet red and yellow became known as the "Kodachrome" scheme among photographers and enthusiasts because of the similar design used by Kodak for the packaging on its slide film. Despite the new livery, and hopes of a unified Southern Pacific and Santa Fe system, the SPSF merger was rejected by the Interstate Commerce Commission in 1986. *Photo by Dave Burton*

Chapter 2

Santa Fe Locomotives

Steam Locomotives

The ubiquitous steam locomotive provided the vast majority of Santa Fe's motive power needs during its first seven decades. Many of Santa Fe's late-era locomotives are considered among the finest examples of steam technology and are remembered today for their outstanding service and performance.

Santa Fe was blessed with a number of coal mines along its lines in Illinois, Kansas, Colorado, and New Mexico, providing its locomotives with adequate fuel. In the twentieth century, following the commercial development of the California oil fields, Santa Fe began using oil-burning locomotives, particularly on its western lines, where the high cost of transporting coal made oil an attractive alternative fuel. In the latter days of steam, oil burners could be found all across its lines, though the lines also used coal-fired locomotives until the late 1950s. Santa Fe was not alone in its widespread use of oil-fired steam, as other western lines, including Southern Pacific and Union Pacific, also operated large fleets of late-era oil burners. Santa Fe bought locomotives from a variety of commercial builders, but also built its own locomotives at company shops. Its modern locomotives, those built during the 1930s and 1940s, were all Baldwin products.

Santa Fe's locomotive classification was distinctive from that of most American railroads. Rather than group similar locomotives by

As Santa Fe dieselized its operations, it gradually sidelined its steam fleet. Often the big locomotives were the first to go. In 1950, Fred Matthews photographed a stored 4-8-2 Mountain-type at Santa Fe's Richmond, California yards. At the time of its retirement, this locomotive had roughly 30 years of service behind it. *Photo by Fred Matthews*

letter type, it simply assigned them a common numbering series and then referred to them by their numeric class based on the first locomotive in the sequence. The railroad generally grouped locomotives of similar characteristics in sequential numbering. For example, its early classes of Pacifics were numbered in the 1200 and 1300 series, while later Pacifics were largely placed in the 3400 and 3500 series. Although Santa Fe's system followed a logical arrangement, it can result in some confusion, especially when the first locomotive of a particular class does not begin at the typical place. Its first class of Hudsons, for example, followed a group of Pacifics, and thus began in the 3450 series.

In the late era, Santa Fe pushed the utilization of steam power to new limits. Traditionally locomotives were exchanged at the end of each district, with districts typically being about 100 miles in length. During World War I, Santa Fe began lengthening the runs of through locomotives and operated them over several consecutive districts. With the success of this practice, the railroad gradually lengthened the maximum run of some locomotives, so by the 1940s, Santa Fe locomotives had some of the longest regular runs in the United States. Its passenger 4-8-4s could operate from Kansas City all the way to Los Angeles, a distance of nearly 1,800 miles.

During World War II, when the railroad was pushed to its maximum capacity, Santa Fe

The 2-10-2 type was a natural evolution from the 2-10-0. On the earliest 2-10-2s, the trailing truck was employed to make reverse movements easier rather than to support a heavy firebox, which was the more common application of a trailing truck. Santa Fe is credited as the first railway to use the 2-10-2 wheel arrangement and, as a result, this arrangement is known as the "Santa Fe" type. This Santa Fe Railway 2-10-2 was one of 74 built by Baldwin between 1905 and 1907. *Photo courtesy of J. R. Quinn*

In the World War I period, the Santa Fe-type became a standard freight hauler on many America railroads. The 3851 seen here was a heavy Santa Fe type, built by Baldwin in the post–World War I period. Baldwin was Santa Fe's primary steam locomotive supplier in the 20th century. *Photo courtesy of J. R. Quinn*

achieved exceptional locomotive utilization. In his book *Railroads at War*, S. Kip Farrington indicates that in July 1942, Santa Fe's passenger locomotives were rolling an average of 318 miles per day, and some locomotives were putting on more than 20,000 miles per month. This extraordinary performance mandated a rigorous and intensive maintenance program.

Early Steam

During the latter half of the nineteenth century, the 4-4-0 American-type was the predominant locomotive on American rails, and the vast majority of Santa Fe's early locomotives were typical 4-4-0s of the period. Santa Fe's first locomotive is usually listed as a secondhand machine acquired from the

Ohio & Mississippi Railroad in 1869, number 1, and named for Santa Fe's founder, *Cyrus K. Holliday*. The well-balanced and versatile design of the 4-4-0 was well suited to a variety of operations and used in both freight and passenger services.

In its early years, Santa Fe's mostly flatland running featured few serious grades and the line had little need for heavier locomotive types. By the 1880s, as Santa Fe reached westward across the mountains of Colorado, New Mexico, Arizona, and California, it acquired larger and heavier locomotives, including 2-8-0 Consolidations and 4-6-0 Ten Wheelers, needed for graded operations. While Santa Fe also bought some 2-6-0 Moguls, this type remained comparatively rare on Santa Fe lines.

In the early years of the twentieth century, Santa Fe purchased large numbers of 4-4-2 Atlantic, and 4-6-2 Pacific types in both simple and compound configurations for its passenger services. The railroad also had a large number of 2-6-2 Prairie types, a type well suited for light lines. The 2-8-0 was a standard freight type all across America and Santa Fe had a great many of them, some inherited though the acquisition of other lines. The 2-8-2 Mikado type was developed for North American service in the early years of the twentieth century. This type eventually became the predominant standard freight locomotive on many American railroads. While Santa Fe ordered a few early Mikados, it did not embrace the type in large numbers until the eve of World War I, a decade after other lines, but then ordered more than 200 of the type.

The growth in passenger traffic combined with the adoption of all-steel passenger equipment resulted in much heavier passenger consists. Following World War I, Santa Fe invested in a fleet of 51 4-8-2 Mountain types to haul these heavier trains. These machines were all built by Baldwin and numbered in the 3700 series.

Compounds

From about 1890 to 1910, American builders promoted compound locomotive designs as a way of achieving greater efficiency. The theory behind a compound is that greater thermal efficiency is achieved by the reuse of exhausted steam. A compound engine employs two sets of cylinders—high-pressure and low-pressure—whereby the high-pressure cylinders exhaust into the low-pressure cylinders, thus extracting more energy from the steam than possible in a conventional simple steam locomotive. Santa Fe, which needed to spend more than average

to provide fuel and suitable water for its western lines, embraced compounding enthusiastically. It employed many compounds using 4-4-2, 4-6-2, and 2-6-2 wheel arrangements. One of the most common types was the Vauclain compound, developed by Baldwin's eccentric Samuel Vauclain. The Vauclain compound was a nonarticulated four-cylinder locomotive that featured a set of both high-pressure and low-pressure cylinders on each side of the locomotive. Santa Fe also used Baldwin's balanced compound types, and Alco-built cross-compounds.

The most unusual aspect of Santa Fe's intrigue with compound steam locomotives was its brief foray with Mallet Articulated types. A Mallet compound is an articulated type that is effectively two engines under a common boiler. In the normal configuration, the rear engine employs high-pressure cylinders that exhaust into the forward engine, which uses low-pressure cylinders. The Mallet was introduced to America in 1904 by the Baltimore & Ohio. The first Mallet was an 0-6-6-0 used in helper service. By 1910 it had found its place as a heavy drag-freight engine, most commonly in the 2-6-6-2 wheel arrangement. Where most railroads that employed Mallets at the time viewed them strictly as low-speed freight engines with small drivers, Santa Fe developed them as relatively high-speed passenger locomotives with tall drivers. Beginning in 1909, Santa Fe employed a variety of non-conventional Mallets and seriously contemplated the construction of some truly fantastic locomotives. It experimented with different wheel arrangements, including two locomotives that employed an unorthodox 4-4-6-2 arrangement. A number of its high-speed Mallets were built with jointed boilers for greater flexibility. In 1911, Santa Fe constructed

Two 2-10-2 Santa Fe-types leading a 4-8-4 approach the Raton Pass tunnel near the Colorado–New Mexico state line with a long passenger train. These 2-10-2s are coal burners, taking advantage of nearby coal reserves. For its lines further west, Santa Fe tended to prefer oil burners to take advantage of the abundance of oil in California. Leading is 3814, one of 140 Baldwin 2-10-2s built following World War I. *Photo by Otto Perry, Denver Public Library, Western History Department, photo OP1973*

ten massive 2-10-10-2s for slow-speed freight service using components from 2-10-2s. At the time, these were the largest locomotives in the world. Most of Santa Fe's Mallets had very short service lives, and some, such as the 2-10-10-2s, were rebuilt as conventional locomotives.

Before it abandoned the articulated type, Santa Fe contemplated the construction of "quadruplex" (2-8-8-8-8-2) and even "quintuplex" (2-8-8-8-8-8-2) types. By the advent of World War I, Santa Fe found that the cost of maintaining a compound locomotive's more complex hardware cancelled out the cost

advantages achieved through improved efficiency. The railroad later rebuilt many compounds into traditional simple engines. However, unlike most western railroads, Santa Fe did not pursue the simple articulated types that became popular in the 1920s.

Santa Fe Type

Santa Fe is credited as being the first railroad to use the 2-10-2 wheel arrangement, and thus this type is known as the "Santa Fe." In 1902, the Santa Fe Railway bought 2-10-0 Decapods for helper service on Raton Pass, but soon found difficulties in operating them for

Streamlined steam was all the rage in the mid-1930s. Santa Fe had just one true steam streamliner, a 4-6-4 Hudson-type with 84-inch tall drivers, No. 3460. This locomotive was adorned in an attractive blue, white, and gray livery and was known as the "Blue Goose". It is seen racing through Medway, Kansas, in 1941 with the Fast Mail Express. *Photo by Otto Perry, Denver Public Library, Western History Department, photo OP1606*

long distances in reverse, and suggested the addition of a rear trailing truck to improve tracking. Santa Fe's first 2-10-2s were built by Baldwin over a four-year span beginning in 1903. Before World War I, Santa Fe ordered additional 2-10-2s followed by a large order for 140 heavy 2-10-2s, after the war. Since a rear trailing truck also helps distribute the weight of the firebox, it allows for the construction of bigger firebox and therefore a more powerful locomotive. Although this was not the original consideration, Santa Fe's later 2-10-2 designs took advantage of the larger firebox. It was this later type that became a standard heavy freight engine on many railroads in North America. Santa Fe made good use of its 2-10-2 as both helper and road freight engines.

Modern Steam

To some readers today, the term "modern steam" may seem incongruous because steam locomotives are often associated with the antique transport of yesteryear, but Santa Fe's late-era steam locomotives were among the most refined and most impressive examples of American steam locomotive design. Even the most hardened proponent of dieseldom should find pause in the study of Santa Fe's modern steam power.

Santa Fe's first modern steam were ten 4-6-4 Hudsons built in 1927. These were built with 73-inch drivers, but later rebuilt with high-pressure boilers and 79-inch drivers. Of greater interest were Santa Fe's six fast "thoroughbred" Hudsons built in 1937 for its premier passenger trains. By this time, Santa Fe had already sampled its first passenger diesels, and these Hudsons needed to be among the best that steam power had to offer in order to rival diesel performance. They had some of the tallest driving wheels of any modern American steam locomotive and measured seven feet high. Numbered in the 3460 series, these Hudsons were built for long-distance high-speed service and regularly ran all the way from Chicago to La Junta, Colorado. In a special publicity run, Santa Fe Hudson 3461 set the world record for the longest continuous steam run, when it operated through from Los Angeles to Chicago on December 9, 1937. The first in this series, No. 3460, was Santa Fe's only fully streamlined steam locomotive. This gorgeous machine was styled in a subtle two-tone blue-and-silver scheme and was colloquially known as the "Blue Goose."

Santa Fe was among the first railroads to adopt the 4-8-4 Northern type and owned the very first Baldwin 4-8-4—No. 3751. These 4-8-4s were bought for passenger service and were normally assigned to work the graded territory west of La Junta. A four-wheel trailing truck enabled the 4-8-4-type to carry a significantly larger firebox than used by the earlier 4-8-2 Mountain type. The larger firebox was key to the Northern's success as an efficient and powerful performer. Santa Fe found that the 3751 series 4-8-4s were significantly more efficient than the Mountains, which it had purchased only a few years earlier. As built, the 3751 class featured 73-inch drivers, but were later rebuilt and modernized with 80-inch drivers.

Some of the finest steam power ever built were Santa Fe's late-era Northerns. Its 2900 class, built during World War II, were massive, but fast machines. They weighed more than a half million pounds, making them the very heaviest 4-8-4s, and were capable of speeds of 100 miles per hour in regular service. The class leader, 2900, is seen racing across the New Mexico desert in the mid-1940s with a 12-car passenger train in tow. *Photo by Otto Perry, Denver Public Library, Western History Department, photo OP1388*

Santa Fe's next class of 4-8-4s, eleven 3765-class, built by Baldwin in 1938, came with large drivers and were built to run through from La Junta to California, a 1,235-mile run.

Santa Fe's last Northerns were its most impressive. The ten 3776-classes in 1940–41, and thirty 2900-classes built during World War II, were magnificent machines with excellent service records. Some were assigned to through passenger service from Kansas City to Los Angeles. The 2900s are often cited as the heaviest Northerns ever built and weighed more than half a million pounds. (Their great weight was partly attributable to wartime restrictions on lightweight alloyed steels.) They were among the fastest big steam and easily capable of reaching 100 miles per hour or more with a long passenger train. Although Santa Fe's 4-8-4s were built primarily for passenger work, many finished out their careers working freight and helper services.

In 1930, Santa Fe took delivery of an experimental Baldwin 2-10-4, Texas type No. 5000, the railroad's first modern locomotive to use that wheel arrangement, but not its first 2-10-4. (In 1919, it had experimented with another locomotive using this arrangement.) Impressed by No. 5000's capabilities, Santa Fe planned to build a fleet of 2-10-4s for freight service but these were delayed by the onset of the Great Depression. It was 1938 before Santa Fe took delivery of its 10 Baldwin-built 5001-class 2-10-4s. These were massive and powerful locomotives with 74-inch drivers, 30x34-inch cylinders, that operated with 310 psi boiler pressure. These large cylinders were some of the largest ever employed by a simple engine and delivered an estimated 210,000 pounds of piston thrust, a statistic credited as the greatest piston thrust of any American locomotive ever built. The

5001s could deliver 93,000 pounds of tractive effort and produce 5,600 horsepower at 40 miles per hour. During the peak traffic period of World War II, Santa Fe took delivery of another 25 Baldwin 2-10-4s, class 5011. These were built in 1944 and were Santa Fe's very last new steam locomotives. These probably would not have been built if wartime limitations had not placed restrictions on diesel locomotive production. Although primarily freight engines, Santa Fe's Texas types were occasionally used in passenger service, and employed to move troop trains during the war.

Santa Fe was among the first railroads to embrace large-scale dieselization and its steam operations wound down rapidly after the war. Yet, pockets of big steam survived into the mid-1950s. One of the last steam operations involved helpers used east of Belen, New Mexico, through Abo Canyon to the summit at Mountainair. The last Santa Fe steam locomotives operated in August 1957; however, the railroad was generous in its preservation of its locomotives and many of its finest were donated to communities along its lines. In 1991, Santa Fe's first 4-8-4, 3751, was restored to active service and in recent years has made occasional trips over former Santa Fe lines.

Early Diesels

A technological antecedent to the first successful road diesels were the self-propelled gas-electric motorcars built in the first two decades of the twentieth century. Santa Fe, like many railroads of the period, bought these gas-electrics for passenger service on branch lines. Santa Fe's cars largely worked secondary lines in Kansas, Oklahoma, Texas, and California. Santa Fe's motorcar fleet included representatives of several builders, including

Brill and General Electric, but the largest number of cars had been the work of the Electro-Motive Corporation (EMC). EMC had entered the railcar business in 1924 and quickly dominated this niche market by the production of high-quality standard models and aggressive marketing techniques. In 1930, General Motors bought both EMC and its engine-supplier, Winton. During the dark days of the Great Depression, General Motors developed America's first diesel-electric streamliners, which were inspired by high-speed diesel trains developed in Germany. The streamliners were an adaptation of EMC's railcar concept using the latest technology and manufacturing techniques. In 1934, EMC's flashy internal combustion–powered articulated streamliners made their debut on Santa Fe's competitors, Burlington and Union Pacific. These trains toured the United States impressing passengers, railroad men, and the press. They inspired a host of streamlined trains on railroads across the United States and effectively created a market for road diesel power.

In the decade prior to the debut of the streamliners, a small market for diesel-electric switchers developed, especially for use in big cities such as New York and Chicago where anti-pollution regulations discouraged the use of steam power. In 1935, Santa Fe bought its first diesel-electric locomotive, an Alco 660 horsepower high-hood locomotive, for service in Chicago. Although intrigued by the sexy attributes of new streamlined trains, Santa Fe was not impressed by the inflexible articulated consists, which it considered impractical for regular service. However, in 1935, EMC demonstrated its early diesel-electric boxcabs on Santa Fe and the railroad purchased a pair of them to haul its new deluxe Chicago–Los Angeles passenger train, the once-weekly *Super*

Chief. Each of these box-cab diesel-electrics was powered by a pair of 900 horsepower Winton 201 diesel engines, giving them a combined output of 3,600 horsepower. They were numbered 1A and 1B, and known by several nicknames, including "The Twins," "Mutt and Jeff," and "Amos 'n' Andy." The boxcabs entered revenue service in 1936, and were rebuilt a couple of years later with a semi-streamlined appearance.

Diesel operation was of special interest to Santa Fe. In addition to greater efficiency offered by the diesel engine and cost savings afforded through reduced fuel and water stops, diesels were attractive because they would simplify its costly mainline desert operations. The lack of suitable water for steam locomotives at many locations on Santa Fe's lines in Arizona and southern California had forced Santa Fe to import water to remote locomotive oases. Poor water quality in the desert also increased operational costs. While Santa Fe's first EMC boxcabs had some operational difficulties, the railroad was sufficiently impressed with their potential to order additional passenger diesels from EMC.

The first of 11 E1A and E1B streamlined diesels were delivered in May 1937 in conjunction with Santa Fe's first streamliner, the Budd-built *Super Chief.* These sleek EMC "E-units" debuted a stylish new paint livery designed by Electro-Motive artist Leland A. Knickerbocker, the legendary scheme now known as the "Warbonnet." This distinctive blend of red, yellow, black, and silver became emblematic of the modern Santa Fe and is unquestionably one of the most recognized railway paint schemes in North America. To maintain its passenger diesel fleet, Santa Fe built a specialized diesel shop at 21st Street in Chicago, perhaps the first such facility in the United States. Santa Fe bought EMC E3s

Santa Fe was an early proponent of Electro-Motive cab units. After it tested EMD's FT set it ordered hundreds of FTs and subsequent EMD cab units for both freight and passenger service. Freight cabs were general painted in blue and yellow, while those in passenger service were dressed in the classic "Warbonnet" livery. Santa Fe F3A 38 leads a passenger train at Chicago in June 1961. *Photo by Richard Jay Solomon*

in 1939, and E6s in 1946. These later E-units were powered by pairs of Electro-Motive 12-cylinder 567 engines—a more powerful and significantly more reliable diesel engine.

Electro-Motive's early success in building passenger and switcher locomotives led to the development of a practical road-freight locomotive, and in 1939 EMC debuted its freight-diesel, a handsomely streamlined machine, today known by its model designation FT. During 1940 and 1941, EMC's freight diesel demonstrator—a four-unit set painted dark green and mustard and rated at 5,400 horsepower—toured the United States, operating on

many different lines, including the Santa Fe. Each of the four units was powered by a 16-cylinder 567 engine rated at 1,350 horsepower, and rode on the recently perfected two-axle Blomberg truck. Santa Fe was among the first users of the FT, and became the largest owner of the model, eventually buying a total of 320 A-units (with cabs) and B-units (cabless "boosters"). These FTs were delivered in a dark blue and yellow livery that contrasted with the flashy Warbonnet scheme used on passenger locomotives. Over the years, Santa Fe used adaptations of the blue and yellow, albeit in more modern schemes, for its freight diesels.

In 1941, General Motors reorganized the Electro-Motive Corporation as its Electro-Motive Division (EMD). In the early days of diesel operation, EMD considered a whole four-unit set as a "locomotive," and it was anticipated that railroads would normally keep sets together. One of the characteristics of the FT model was semi-permanently coupled A- and B-unit sets. Santa Fe found this arrangement unsatisfactory for the same reasons it shunned articulated passenger trains: semi-permanently coupled consists hampered flexibility. So, Santa Fe's FT locomotives were not permanently coupled, and ultimately its philosophy prevailed, as EMD discontinued the semi-permanently coupled concept on postwar models.

Santa Fe initially assigned its FTs to work between Winslow, Arizona, and terminals at Barstow and Bakersfield, California. This became one of the world's first predominantly diesel-powered mainlines. The operating characteristics of the FT were ideal for this rigorous territory where long, stiff grades, poor water, and extreme summer heat combined to make steam operations difficult and expensive. Initially, a diesel shop was established at Winslow, with fueling facilities at Seligman, Arizona, and Needles and Barstow, California. The FTs were used to supplant 2-10-2s on heavy freight and, according to S. Kip Farrington in his *Railroads at War,* they were allowed to handle trains up to 3,500 tons in both directions over the Arizona Divide. Employing FTs simplified operations and speeded train movements since FTs needed far fewer fuel and water stops than steam power, while the FT's high-traction capabilities at slow speeds negated the need for helpers in many locations. Furthermore, the use of the FT's dynamic brakes greatly improved train handling and saved on the wear of brakeshoes. Farrington notes in his *Railroading from the Head End* that a diesel-powered freight operating from Chicago to the Pacific coast needed to make just five fuel stops, compared with 18 or 19 fuel stops, and between 34 and 36 water stops, required for a typical steam-powered train of the same period.

Postwar Dieselization

During World War II, Santa Fe's FT fleet greatly helped keep the heavy flow of freight traffic moving over its lines. Yet, the war made it difficult for Santa Fe (as well as other lines) to procure new diesel power. Following the war, Santa Fe resumed its large-scale dieselization with the purchase of additional F-units. Over the following decade, Santa Fe acquired nearly 450 additional postwar F-units, some for use in both freight and passenger service. The last Fs were a batch of 35 F9s rated at 1,750 horsepower, acquired in 1956 for freight service. Some of the FTs were later modified for passenger duties, regeared and repainted into the Warbonnet scheme. Generally speaking, the passenger Fs were in Warbonnet while freight units were dressed in variations of the blue and yellow.

The Warbonnet F-Unit will remain the most familiar of all Santa Fe locomotives because of its popularity with model and toy train manufacturers. Since Lionel first brought out the Santa Fe F3 in O Scale in 1948, tens of thousands of miniature Santa Fe Fs have thrilled children of all ages around the globe. The effects on public consciousness should not be discounted—the toy Warbonnet has helped make the Santa Fe one of the most popular of all railroads. This popularity in turn inspired Santa Fe officers to revive the Warbonnet livery for road locomotives in 1989.

The majority of Santa Fe's early diesel acquisition was focused on EMD products. Among the exceptions were the aforementioned first switcher, and a pair of Alco cabs, (models DL109 and DL110) that were built for passenger service. In the postwar steam-to-diesel transition period, Santa Fe spread its orders among all the major diesel builders, but continued to favor EMD for the largest share of its road locomotives. In addition to the large numbers of EMD Fs, Santa Fe bought nearly 300 EMD "Geeps" (GP7s and GP9s, rated at 1,500 horsepower and 1,750 horsepower, respectively). These locomotives were EMD's successful road switchers that dominated the domestic market through the 1950s. Santa Fe also bought many EMD, switchers including models SC, NW2, SW9, and SW1200.

Baldwin, which had been Santa Fe's primary steam supplier, provided some switchers mostly VO1000s rated at 1,000 horsepower, and a few road-switchers, including six-motor DT-6-6-2000s (that were later traded to General Electric), but did not play a major role in Santa Fe's dieselization. Baldwin's road diesels did not fare well against those built by Alco and EMD, and were generally not well regarded. By contrast, its World War II-era switchers were considered good machines.

In 1944, diesel-engine manufacturer and railway equipment supplier Fairbanks-Morse (F-M) chose to enter the heavy diesel-electric locomotive business as a postwar outlet for its engines. It had perfected an opposed-piston design that had proved well suited for marine applications. However, Fairbanks-Morse, like Baldwin, found it difficult to compete effectively in the new diesel market. Even during the height of the steam-to-diesel transition period when railroads were scrambling for new diesel power, F-M sold only a small fraction of locomotives in comparison with EMD, and by the mid-1950s, F-M effectively exited the locomotive business. Santa Fe operated a small fleet of F-Ms. It had a single three-unit set of F-M "Erie-built" cab units built in 1947 that were dressed in Warbonnet and worked passenger trains. Although less noticeable, Santa Fe also operated more than 80 F-M switchers and road-switcher models.

Alco supplied a fair number of Santa Fe locomotives in the 1940s and 1950s. Certainly the highest-profile Alco diesels were its 44 Alco PA/PBs bought in 1946 for passenger work. Each PA/PB unit was rated at 2,000 horsepower using a 16-cylinder 244 engine. Like other passenger diesels, the PA/PBs were dressed in Warbonnet, and with their six-foot-long nose section have long been considered one of the most attractive diesel designs by locomotive enthusiasts. The PAs were not as reliable as EMD Fs, and generally were assigned to secondary trains such as the *Grand Canyon,* and mail trains. They were mostly retired during 1968 and 1969, but four Santa Fe PAs were bought by Delaware & Hudson, where they worked for another decade before being sent to Mexico. In recent years, two of the ex-Santa Fe PAs have been repatriated to from Mexico for restoration and possible excursion work. Santa Fe operated a large number of Alco switchers and road switchers, including some HH1000s, dozens of S2s, a half-dozen 1,000 horsepower RS-1s, 63 six- motor RSD-4s and RSD-5s, as well as 12 RSD-7s and 50 RSD-15s, 2,250 and 2,400 horsepower six-motor units built between 1955 and 1960.

Despite the relatively large orders for 1950s-era high-horsepower locomotives, Santa Fe abandoned Alco entirely in the 1960s and never bought any of Alco's Century-series high-horsepower models. Instead, after 1960

In 1983, a pair of GP20s lead a local freight across the diamonds at Brighton Park, Chicago, Illinois. Brighton Park is one of the last non-interlocked railroad-level crossings in the United States. The semaphores are manually operated from the small building to the left of the train. *Photo by Steve Smedley*

Santa Fe began sampling General Electric diesels. Alco and GE worked together in the diesel business until 1953, when this arrangement was dissolved and GE embarked on the development of its own heavy road-diesel designs. GE's Universal Line made its debut in 1960, and by the mid-1980s, GE surpassed EMD as America's largest locomotive manufacturer. By the early 1990s, GE had become Santa Fe's primary locomotive supplier.

High-Horsepower Diesels

During the 1950s, as railroads, including Santa Fe, completed dieselization, the market for new locomotives declined. In order to generate further sales in a saturated market, the remaining locomotive manufacturers perfected their designs' reliability, while increasing the per-unit horsepower available on individual models. Diesels afforded railroads many operational and cost advantages over steam. But by the late 1950s and early 1960s, the big western carriers were keen to obtain even greater operational savings through the operation of much longer and heavier trains. To accomplish this, Santa Fe's competitors, UP and SP, embraced some unconventional motive power schemes: Union Pacific bought a fleet of very high horsepower General Electric gas turbines,

On May 10, 1988, Santa Fe GP30 2723 leads a westbound through Edelstein, Illinois. Santa Fe rebuilt its GP30s and operated them for many years after other railroads had forsaken the model. *Photo by Mike Danneman*

while Southern Pacific experimented with diesel hydraulics to obtain greater power, importing Krauss-Maffeis from Germany and trying domestic hydraulics from Alco. In the early 1960s, both UP and SP bought high-horsepower double-diesels. Meanwhile, Santa Fe embraced less radical high-horsepower schemes.

In the late 1950s, Santa Fe ordered the latest high-horsepower diesels from Alco and EMD. In addition to the Alco models already discussed, Santa Fe bought a fleet of eighty 2,400

horsepower six-motor EMD SD24s, and in 1960–61 seventy-five EMD 2,000 horsepower four-motor GP20s. These two models were different from all earlier EMDs as they employed 567-engines with a turbocharger in the place of the Roots blower, in order to obtain greater horsepower. Between 1962 and 1966, Santa Fe bought more EMD high-horsepower four-motor units with eighty-five 2,250 horsepower GP30s, followed by one hundred sixty-one 2,500 horsepower GP35s. Santa Fe retired its original FT fleet as it acquired these high-horsepower units and EMD recycled some components, such as the FT's Blomberg trucks, which rode beneath the GP20s, GP30s, and GP35s. High-powered four-motor models were well suited to Santa Fe's style of long-distance fast-freight operations and Santa Fe would continue to buy new high-horsepower four-motor diesels until the early 1990s. Santa Fe also sampled General Electric's road diesels, acquiring the first of GE's recently introduced Universal line by taking delivery of 16 U25Bs (rated at 2,500 horsepower) during 1962 and 1963.

Santa Fe bought many six-motor locomotives for heavy freight service during the 1960s and 1970s. In 1966, it acquired 20 EMD SD40s. This 3,000 horsepower locomotive was one of nine new models debuted in 1965. In addition to a newly designed 645 engine that was both more powerful and more reliable than EMD's 567 engine, these new locomo-

tives featured a host of significant improvements, including a new electrical system and improved electrical components. Of the most impressive 645-models was the very powerful SD45, rated at 3,600 horsepower, which proved an immediate sensation on big western railroads. Great Northern bought the first SD45, and soon Northern Pacific, Burlington, Union Pacific, Southern Pacific, and Frisco, as well as some eastern lines, were using fleets of SD45s. Santa Fe bought 125 of them between 1966 and 1970—just less than 10 percent of the total SD45 production run. Santa Fe received good service from the 20-cylinder 645 engine and, in addition to its SD45 fleet, ordered several other models with this engine, including cowl types discussed below, and 90 SD45-2s. EMD's "Dash-2" model lines, introduced in 1972, had the same primary characteristics (and designations) as their

A pair of SD45s and a pair of SD40s lead a westbound at Caliente, California, on January 29, 1976. The 3,600 horsepower SD45 was the most powerful single-engine machine on the market when introduced in 1965. The low bass roar of the 20-cylinder 645 engine was a common sound on Santa Fe rails for three decades. Santa Fe had one of the largest and longest lived SD45 fleets—125 units—and also operated FP45s, F45s, and SD45-2s, all of which used the big engine. *Photo by Brian Jennison*

Left: The short-lived SPSF 'merger' scheme is worn by four Santa Fe locomotives shown working eastbound over the Tehachapis at Marcel, California, on March 10, 1988. By this time the SPSF merger had been rejected by the ICC, and Santa Fe had discontinued painting locomotives in this livery. Leading is F45 5976, followed by SD45 5380, and a pair of General Electric C30-7s. *Photo by Brian Jennison*

Below: With 90 units, Santa Fe had by far the largest roster of EMD SD45-2s, the 20-cylinder 3,600 horsepower model that succeeded the SD45. Unlike its predecessor, the SD45-2 did not require the characteristic tapered or "flared" radiators, and thus it closely resembled the more common SD40-2. In the spirit of America's Bicentennial, Santa Fe dressed SD45-2 5701 in a patriotic livery. On January 31, 1976, it leads an eastbound over Cajon Pass against a backdrop of the San Gabriels. *Photo by Brian Jennison*

On October 21, 1979, a clean new SD40-2 5110 leads an eastbound freight through the Warren Curve near Mojave, California. Between 1977 and 1981, Santa Fe acquired just under 200 SD40-2s. This model was one of the most popular diesels of all time and has earned praise from railroaders as one of the best locomotives on the road. Many are still in service today. *Photo by Brian Jennison*

predecessor models but featured an improved electrical system and other component improvements such as higher adhesion trucks.

The SD40-2 and SD45-2 were basically improved variations of the SD40 and SD45 respectively. The horsepower ratings remained consistent. However, by the time the Dash-2 line debuted, the 3,600 horsepower SD45, had fallen out of favor, making Santa Fe's fleet SD45-2 unusual because it was one of the largest Dash-2 applications of the 20-cylinder 645 engine. Southern Pacific was the other large user of the type with its large fleet of SD45T-2s, a model that featured a substantially altered airflow pattern to accommodate prolonged operation in tunnels at high altitudes. The most popular Dash-2 model was the 3,000 horsepower SD40-2, which quickly became a ubiquitous symbol of modern railroading. According to *The Contemporary Diesel Spotter's Guide* by Louis A. Marre

and Paul K. Withers, 3,126 SD40-2s were built for domestic lines, and hundreds more for use in Canada and Mexico. Santa Fe bought 197 SD40-2s, making them one of the most common modern units in its road fleet. Yet, Santa Fe's fleet was relatively small in comparison to those operated by Union Pacific and Burlington Northern.

Santa Fe acquired many high-horsepower six-motor locomotives from General Electric, although generally in smaller quantities than from EMD. Santa Fe first bought 25 U33Cs in 1969 and 1970, followed by 106 U36Cs in the mid-1970s, and 157 C30-7s in the late 1970s.

Rebuilds and Road-Switchers

Santa Fe's locomotives were characterized by long and productive careers. Among the features that distinguish Santa Fe's diesel fleet from other large North American railroads were Santa Fe's superb maintenance practices

and homemade rebuilds. While some other lines chewed through motive power, providing minimal maintenance and routinely making large purchases for new locomotives as they disposed of worn-out machines, Santa Fe recycled old locomotives rather than scrapping them.

Santa Fe's aggressive program of rebuilding its old locomotives contributed to their longevity. In 1970, as its large F7 fleet was reaching retirement age, Santa Fe began the remanufacture of these locomotives at its Cleburne, Texas, shops, turning them into homemade road-switchers, known as CF7s. After a decade of service on the Santa Fe, many of the CF7s were sold to shortlines around the country, where today many are still running. The CF7 program was just the beginning and Santa Fe subsequently rebuilt its fleet of GP7s, GP20s, GP30s, and GP35s, among others. By the mid-1990s, these locomotives could still be found in mainline and local service around its system, a full decade after they had completely disappeared from other

Above: Santa Fe SD26 4611 rests outside the Bakersfield Roundhouse on February 15, 1979. Santa Fe purchased 80 SD24s, EMD's first turbocharged high-horsepower six-motor diesel. Between 1973 and 1978, Santa Fe rebuilt its SD24 fleet, making significant modifications to the locomotives, including the replacement of the original 16-cylinder 567 engine with the more modern (and more reliable) 16-645E, which boosted locomotive output to 2,650 horsepower. *Photo by Brian Jennison*

Right top: This Santa Fe-rebuilt GP35 2938 leads a quartet of four-motor EMDs with a westbound freight out of the railroad's sprawling Barstow, California, yard. Santa Fe's diverse roster of modern locomotives was among the most eclectic of the large American railroads in the 1990s. This can be in part attributed to Santa Fe's excellent maintenance, which kept older and unusual models running much longer than on other lines. *Photo by Brian Solomon*

Right bottom: Idling in the cold under the greenish glow of mercury-vapor yard lamps, CF7 2571 sits near the sand tower in Oklahoma City's Nowers Yard awaiting assignment four days before Christmas in 1979. One of a total 132 units, this homemade road-switcher was built in the railroad's Cleburne, Texas, shops in May 1973 from F7A 202L. No. 2571 was sold to the Los Angeles Junction Railway in 1984. Servicing was moved south of town to the new Flynn Yard in the early 1980s and the service area here was leveled. *Photo by Tom Kline*

In 1964 and 1965, Santa Fe bought EMD's 2,500 horsepower GP35 for fast intermodal work. They had long and productive lives working for Santa Fe. GP35 3350 leads a westbound at Cajon Summit on March 30, 1979. In later years, rebuilt GP35s were common power on local and branch line freights. *Photo by Don Marson*

companys' mainlines. The rebuilding and re-manufacture of EMD locomotives became a fairly common practice in the railroad industry; however, beginning in 1985, Santa Fe took the very unusual step of rebuilding many of its U36C fleet at its Cleburne shops. Santa Fe's rebuilt U36Cs emerged from the rebuild program as 3,000 horsepower SF30Cs, giving

them another decade of useful service.

Santa Fe also purchased moderately powered locomotives from both EMD and GE, including 2,000 horsepower GP38s, 2,300 horsepower GP39s and SD39s. The latter two models used turbocharged 12-cylinder engines. From GE, Santa Fe bought four-motor 2,300 horsepower U23Bs and six-motor 2,300

A spring rain has just started to fall, streaking the nose and pilot of SF30C 9552 as it wheels around a curve into Bellville, Texas, with G-KCHO (Grain: Kansas City–Houston) on March 10, 1990. Santa Fe made an unusual decision to rebuild its old General Electric diesels. This Santa Fe locomotive began life as a GE U36C and was rebuilt into a homemade model by Santa Fe at its Cleburne shops in July 1986. During a one-year production run, the electricians and machinists at Cleburne turned out a total of 70 SF30Cs. *Photo by Tom Kline*

Santa Fe C30-7 8159 shines in the sun at Davidson, Texas, wearing the "yellowbonnet" paint scheme adopted in 1972 for all freight units. A total of 157 of these units were purchased for their heavy-haul lugging capability and served the Santa Fe for more than 20 years. This unit is leading an empty unit grain train up from the port of Galveston on the subdivision of the same name. After changing crews several towns away in Temple, the train will continue north to the grain belt to be reloaded and return to back to the docks along the Gulf of Mexico. *Photo by Tom Kline*

horsepower U23Cs, and later, four-motor B23-7s, an improved version of the U23B.

Cowl Locomotives

GE built the first cowls in 1967 with six U30CGs for passenger service. Earlier, GE had built conventional-looking U28CGs dressed in Warbonnet for Santa Fe passenger service.

In 1968, EMD built nine FP45s for Santa Fe. These locomotives were basically a covered version of the SD45 with a large steam generator for passenger service (in the 1960s, American passenger trains still used steam for train heat, a carryover from the steam era). They used the 20-cylinder 645 and were rated at 3,600 horsepower. Although not stream-

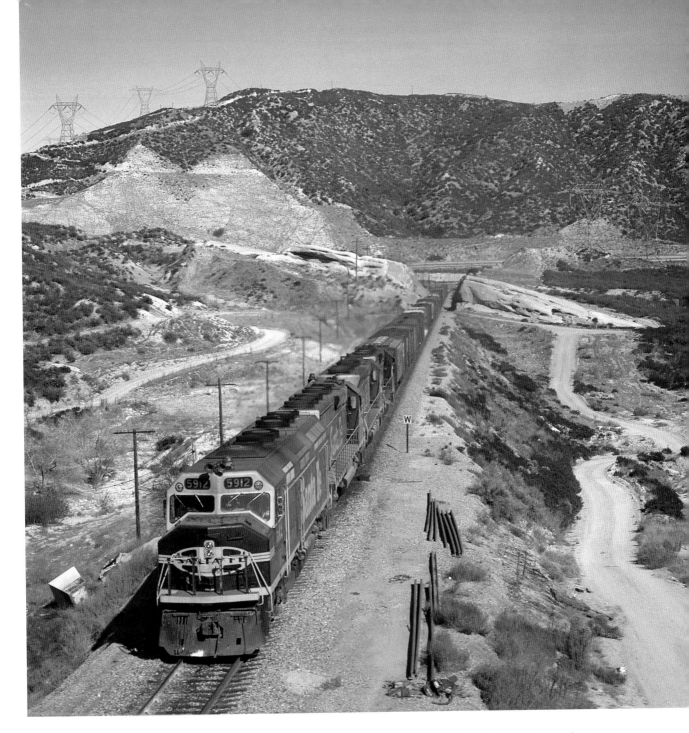

Santa Fe's 40 F45s were built by EMD between 1968 and 1970. In most respects these were similar to the FP45; however, they were not equipped with the large steam generator for passenger service and as a result are roughly five feet shorter. Santa Fe F45 5912 leads an eastbound freight out of Cajon siding on January 31, 1976. *Photo by Brian Jennison*

lined in the style of the Es and Fs, the FP45 featured a more attractive overall appearance than contemporary road switchers. The front-end featured a widenose-cab design and cleaner lines than the typical EMDs of the period. Satisfied with this design, Santa Fe ordered another 40 EMD cowls for freight service designated as F45s. These did not use the large steam generator. In 1984, Santa Fe acquired 18 additional cowls, model SDP40Fs, from Amtrak that were rated at 3,000 horsepower. The GE U30CGs were only briefly used in passenger service and only lasted little more

Right: Santa Fe GP60M 119 leads a westbound through the Bealville Horseshoe in the California Tehachapis on March 29, 1992. Santa Fe's GP60Ms were the first modern four-axle locomotives for the American market equipped with safety cabs, they were also the only modern EMD four-axle locomotives with safety cabs. Santa Fe had difficulty with its GP60Ms in the Tehachapis, and preferred to assign its GE B40-8BWs to priority intermodal trains on this route. *Photo by Brian Solomon*

Below: The afternoon shadows encroach on the narrow defile known as Abo Canyon, New Mexico, as a Santa Fe intermodal train snakes its way westward. Santa Fe's Warbonnet-painted "Super Fleet" was normally assigned to high-priority intermodal trains. Leading this train are three General Electric DASH 8s, and a sole FP45. *Photo by Brian Solomon*

Following pages: In 1994, Santa Fe received its last new General Electric locomotives, 100 DASH 9-44CWs, Nos. 600 to 699. The DASH 9 line reflected a number of improvements to GE's product line, including electronic fuel injection, "split cooling," and a new style of truck that provided higher adhesion. Santa Fe's DASH 9s were rated at 4,400 horsepower, making them the most powerful locomotives on the railroad. DASH 9-44CW 617 and DASH 8-40CW 849 lead an eastbound near Ancona, Illinois. *Photo by Brian Solomon*

Above: Not all late-era Santa Fe locomotives were painted in the Warbonnet livery. Switchers, such as this MK1200G built by MK Rail at Boise, Idaho, in 1994, were delivered in blue and yellow. In the mid-1990s, Santa Fe experimented with locomotives fueled by liquefied natural gas for reduced engine exhaust emissions. *Photo by Don Marson*

than a decade in freight service. By contrast, many of Santa Fe's FP45s and F45s were still working in the mid-1990s, and many even outlasted the Santa Fe.

High-Tech Locomotives and Super Fleet

In the late 1970s and early 1980s, Santa Fe acquired the latest modern, high-horsepower four-motor locomotives for service hauling its fast intermodal trains. The first of these were 10 GP40Xs, what is often considered an experimental model that was rated at 3,500 horsepower. This model was equipped with the latest wheel-slip system. Santa Fe was one of just four railroads to get new GP40Xs, the other three being Union Pacific, Southern Pacific, and Southern Railway. In 1980, EMD debuted its "Super Series," and over the next five years Santa Fe acquired a fleet of 45 GP50s, which were powered by a 16-cylinder 645F engine rated at 3,500 horsepower. In 1985, EMD's GP50 was superseded by the GP60, a model that used EMD's higher-displacement 16-710G engine rated at 3,800 horsepower, which also proved significantly more reliable than the 16-645F. Santa Fe bought 40 GP60s.

During this period, Santa Fe bought 16 U36Bs from General Electric in 1980. In 1984, General Electric assigned three B39-8s to the Santa Fe. This was one of four small fleets of "pre-production" locomotives GE built for road testing new microprocessor technology on North American lines. Initially, General Electric retained ownership of the B39-8s. Later, Santa Fe acquired 40 production-built DASH 8-40Bs.

Modern American road locomotives had evolved from the road-switcher type of the late 1940s. However, the cab and control stand arrangement that made sense for a 1940s-era road switcher was deemed inadequate for modern operations where locomotive engineers faced forward for hours at a time. To address this issue, Santa Fe was instrumental in the development of the North American Safety Cab, which was intended to provide a more ergonomic work environment for crews. In 1988, Santa Fe surveyed its locomotive crews and tested a modern Canadian National SD50F that featured the latest version of the Canadian "widenose" cab design. Although Union Pacific's SD60Ms were the first American locomotives delivered with North American Safety Cabs, Santa Fe's 63 GP60Ms

built in 1990 and numbered in the 100-series, also incorporated this "new" design.

While the Safety Cab involved many changes in cab design, its antecedents can clearly be seen in both the "Cowl" locomotives of the 1960s (including Santa Fe's FP45s) and modern Canadian locomotives. The debut of the GP60M coincided with Santa Fe's decision, under the direction of President Mike Haverty, to re-adopt the popular Warbonnet paint livery for its "Super Fleet" locomotives used to haul its premier intermodal trains. During the summer of 1989, as a prelude to the delivery of the GP60Ms, Santa Fe repainted its FP45 fleet in the vibrant Warbonnet. Santa Fe was the only railroad to order the GP60M, and the only American freight railroad to use modern high-horsepower four-motor locomotives with Safety Cabs. For that matter, Santa Fe was among the very last American freight railroads to order high-horsepower four-motor locomotives of any type, because by the early 1990s the type had largely fallen out of favor. No high-horsepower four-motor locomotives have been built for freight service since 1994.

Following the GP60Ms came an order for 59 General Electric DASH 8-40BWs numbered in the 500-series which, like the GP60Ms, came with Safety Cabs and were initially assigned to Santa Fe's highest-priority intermodal services such as the 199/991 United Parcel trains. In 1991, Santa Fe placed its last order for four-motor locomotives with 23 cab-less GP60Bs from EMD. This unusual order of modern B-units has been attributed to the very high cost of modern Safety Cabs and the fact that high-horsepower locomotives like the GP60 were typically run in sets of four or more units.

Modern high-tech six-motor GEs joined the Super Fleet beginning in 1992. Since the late

In September 1995, Santa Fe received its last new locomotive, EMD SD75 250, before the consummation of the merger with Burlington Northern. On September 5, 1995, Santa Fe arranged for Tom Danneman and Brian Solomon, then working for *Pacific RailNews*, to photograph the locomotive at the Corwith diesel shop in Chicago. *Photo by Brian Solomon and Tom Danneman*

1970s, Santa Fe had focused its locomotive acquisitions on four-motor types, and had thus missed a whole generation of six-motor locomotives. It never bought any EMD SD50s or SD60s and its first modern six-motor locomotives were a fleet of GE DASH 8-40CWs numbered in the 800 and 900 series. According to *Diesel Era* magazine, these locomotives were delivered with a 3,800 horsepower rating at Santa Fe's request (instead of the standard 4,000 horsepower rating), and rode on 42-inch wheels, instead of the more common 40-inch wheels. Since Santa Fe intended some of the locomotives for its York Canyon coal service, where coal-loading equipment posed dimensional restrictions, all of its six-motor GEs featured a different cab roofline profile than other GE Safety cabs. The units specifically assigned to coal service were also equipped with slow-speed motor controls needed for loading trains. Santa Fe's later six-motor DASH-8s, 25 units beginning with locomotive 935, were built with an improved radiator design known as "Split Cooling." As a result, locomotives had a slightly higher output and were rated at 4,135 horsepower and, accordingly, are sometimes designated DASH 8-41CW.

In 1993, General Electric's DASH 9 line was introduced to supersede its DASH 8 line. This was essentially a marketing move made to reflect a host of design improvements to the GE product line, some of which, like "Split Cooling," had already been implemented on late-era DASH 8s. Santa Fe received 100 DASH 9s in 1994. These were numbered in the 600-series and featured GE's new Hi-Ad truck, which makes them easily distinguishable from the DASH 8s.

Santa Fe's final class of locomotives were ordered after the merger with BN had been announced. These were 50 SD75Ms numbered 200 to 250 built by EMD beginning in March 1995. They were rated at 4,300 horsepower. According to Steve Glischinski in his *Santa Fe Railway*, the output of five SD75s was boosted to 4,500 horsepower as an experiment. The very last new Santa Fe locomotive, SD75M 250, was delivered to the railroad's Corwith Yard on September 4, 1995, less than three weeks before the Santa Fe would merge with BNSF. Additional SD75Ms were later received by BNSF.

Santa Fe 250 was brand-new when photographed on September 5, 1995. Although the railroad name would disappear into the corporate wash of BNSF, the Warbonnet livery survived a little longer as several subsequent orders of BNSF locomotives were delivered in Warbonnet paint. *Photo by Brian Solomon and Tom Danneman*

Chapter 3

Santa Fe Operations

Passenger Service

Limiteds, Expresses, and Chiefs

In Santa Fe's first 100 years, passenger trains were integral to its operations and one of the defining elements of the railroad in the public eye. Its famous long-distance trains set standards for speed, service, and quality. The famed *California Limited* connecting Chicago and Los Angeles debuted in 1892. In its early years, this train was Santa Fe's first-class flagship to the West Coast. By the turn of the twentieth century, the *California Limited* was a rolling luxurious display of Victorian-era splendor and one of the finest trains in the West. According to Keith L. Bryant Jr. in his *History of the Atchison, Topeka and Santa Fe Railway*, at this time the *California Limited* would have normally carried three Pullman sleepers, a diner, and a buffet/smoking car. Bryant also notes that in the period from 1897 to 1917, Santa Fe enjoyed a 600 percent rise in its passenger traffic.

Although Santa Fe variously operated other Chicago–California trains such as the Chicago–San Francisco *San Francisco Express* and *Chicago Express* and the Chicago-Los Angeles *Los Angeles Express* and *Atlantic Express*, at times of heavy traffic the *California Limited* would operate in multiple sections to accommodate the heavy tide of passengers. Running passenger services in "sections" was a common railroad operating practice in times when traffic exceeded the capacity of single train. Each section was a full train operating with an engine

A westbound Santa Fe intermodal train glides through Christie, California, just a few miles from its terminus at Richmond. It's spring, the grass is an iridescent green, and the mustard flowers are blooming. Soon the fog will burn off, and the bright California sun will illuminate Franklin Canyon. *Photo by Brian Solomon*

A hand painted period postcard depicts Santa Fe's California Limited passing Joshua trees in the Mojave desert. A pair of 4-4-0s lead Santa Fe's premier turn-of-the-century passenger run. *John Gruber collection*

and cars that operated on the same timetable as the regularly scheduled train. Typically, sections followed each other closely in rapid succession over the railroad. Extra sections would sometimes operate in advance of the schedule. The "extras" would be identified by green classification markers (flags or lamps) in order to alert railroad employees that additional sections were following.

Beginning in December 1911, Santa Fe offered an exceptionally luxurious and thoroughly exclusive train called the *Santa Fe De-Luxe*. It ran just once a week and catered to a limited number of passengers. Period advertising states that the train accommodated just 60 people. By the standards of the day it was extraordinarily expensive and carried a $25 extra-fare above the cost of a regular first-class ticket. The Santa Fe *De-Luxe* was to transcontinental railway travel what the *Concorde* is to transatlantic air travel today. According to Bryant, the *De-Luxe* trimmed between five-and-a-half to seven hours 45 minutes off the Chicago to Los Angeles run, making it much faster than the *California Limited*. Passengers were treated with a variety of luxuries, including barber services, a library, and telephone connections at major stations. While today we take for granted mobile phones and modern communications, having phones on board a train at stations would have been considered the epitome of modern convenience in 1911. The *De-Luxe* and some other Santa Fe named trains, such as the overnight *Saint* and *Angel* that connected San Francisco and Los Angeles, were canceled with American involvement in World War I.

In the 1920s, patronage on Santa Fe's passenger services started to suffer competition

Santa Fe took great pride in its passenger terminals. Its San Diego station was built in 1915 at the time of the California-Pacific Exposition, a large fair celebrating the completion of the Panama Canal. The station blended Spanish and Moorish architectural styles and incorporated the railroad's logo in mosaic tiles on the roofs of towers that flanked the main structure. *Photo by Brian Solomon*

Santa Fe was one of the first American railroads to use streamlined diesel locomotives and cars in passenger service. The streamlined Super Chief debuted in 1937 and provided an extra-fare first class service between Chicago and Los Angeles. This hand colored view of Electro-Motive Corporation model E1A and E1B diesels with a Budd-built streamlined cars was used on company brochures and postcards. *Santa Fe postcard, Richard Jay Solomon collection*

SANTA FE STREAMLINER EN ROUTE BETWEEN CHICAGO AND CALIFORNIA

Santa Fe's Alco PAs were built for long-distance passenger service. The railroad owned 28 PAs and 16 PB cabless boosters. An A-B-A set of the Alcos are seen racing westward across the plains of eastern Colorado with one of Santa Fe's secondary long-distance passenger trains, probably the Northern section of the *Grand Canyon,* which in January 1956 was scheduled to stop at La Junta, Colorado, at 8:05 AM. *Photo by Otto Perry, Denver Public Library Western History Department, photo OP2196*

from private automobiles (and, to a much lesser extent, commercial aircraft). Secondary lines and rural branches were hardest hit, but long-distance traffic was affected too. In order to attract passengers back, Santa Fe offered improved services and launched intensive advertising campaigns. In addition to promoting its own trains, it renewed efforts to encourage tourism in the Southwest, enticing people to visit the Grand Canyon, Carlsbad Caverns, and Native American rituals.

In November 1926, Santa Fe reintroduced a fast, exclusive, luxurious Chicago–Los Angeles service with a train named the *Chief,* which operated on a daily schedule, rather than a weekly one. Like its predecessor, the *De-Luxe,* the *Chief* offered passengers a very high quality of service provided at an extra-fare of $10 above ticket cost. Passengers were treated to onboard bathing facilities, barber services, and other amenities that would appeal to a better class of passenger. Speedy service was also stressed, and the *Chief* was expedited over the railroad on especially fast schedules. By 1930, the train was running on a regular 56-hour schedule from Chicago to L.A. During the 1930s, Santa Fe also introduced air-conditioning to this service in dining cars and lounges. Cool air was undoubtedly appreciated by passengers crossing the scorching Southwestern deserts in summer.

To attract budget-minded travelers, Santa Fe offered secondary-named trains at more reasonable fares, that provided a good quality service. These trains supplemented the long-running *California Limited,* offering transcontinental passengers a choice of departure times, as well as routing options. The *Navajo* served Santa Fe's preferred passenger route by way of La Junta, Colorado, and Albuquerque while the *Scout* operated on a southerly transcontinental routing by way of Amarillo, Texas, and the Belen Cutoff. In 1929, Santa Fe introduced its *Grand Canyon Limited*, which became one of its most popular trains, a long-distance stopping service that served many small on-line communities, yet provided a high-quality sleeping car and coach accommodation. At Williams, Arizona, the *Grand Canyon* dropped cars providing a through-service to its namesake.

In November 1936, Santa Fe introduced its most famous train, the legendary *Super Chief,* a premium-class, super-fast, deluxe Chicago–L.A service. Initially a weekly service, provided with Santa Fe's finest heavyweight sleepers hauled by new diesel-electric boxcabs, the *Super Chief* sprinted across the country on an amazing 39 hour 45 minute end-to-end schedule. It was *Super Chief's* new diesels—motive power that required fewer fuel and water stops than steam—that made this run possible.

Santa Fe Streamliners

Burlington's diesel-powered stainless steel *Zephyr*, introduced in 1934, had captured the attention of the traveling public. Santa Fe officials were impressed by the train's promise, but not keen on its cramped accommodations and inflexible articulated consist. Following the debut and success of Santa Fe's own diesel-powered *Super Chief,* the railroad turned to Budd and Electro-Motive for the design and construction of a diesel-powered streamlined train that would embody the best qualities of Burlington's *Zephyr* trains and conventional ones. Santa Fe wanted the speed and sex appeal of the *Zephyr* while retaining the traditional flexibility of conventionally coupled cars, and the space and comfort provided by

Los Angeles Union Passenger Terminal was the last classic large railway terminal built in the United States. It replaced earlier stations and served all three of the major railroads in Los Angeles: Southern Pacific, Union Pacific and, of course, Santa Fe. This was where passengers would board Santa Fe's most famous trains—the *Chief, Super Chief,* and *El Capitan*—for points east. Many a movie star began or ended his or her rail journey here. *Photo by Brian Solomon*

full-sized passenger equipment. This is exactly what Santa Fe got in its all-new streamlined *Super Chief,* which debuted in May 1937.

Super Chief was a trendsetter in 1930s style. Where Burlington had used classical themes with its *Zephyrs*, Santa Fe subtlety blended traditional Southwestern motifs with the latest in railway designs and technology to produce a classy, distinctive, and original streamliner. The train's styling was the work of Paul F. Cret, S. B. McDonald, and Santa Fe's advertising executive, Roger W. Birdseye. Each of the

train's cars featured a slightly different interior style based on traditional Native American themes. In its first month, the *Super Chief* was hauled by Santa Fe's EMC boxcabs then, in June 1937, the first EMC streamlined E1 diesels in the famous Warbonnet paint took over. Response to this stunning new streamliner was outstanding. The *Super Chief* more than any other train defined Santa Fe's corporate image for decades to come, and it became one of the most famous of all American trains. For a generation, it was *the* choice of passage to the West Coast by Hollywood

An EA-EB set leads Santa Fe's *Golden Gate* from Bakersfield to Oakland, California. It is the summer of 1947 and the train is pulling around the last curve into Santa Fe's 40th & San Pablo station in Emeryville. From here, San Francisco-bound passengers will catch a railroad bus over the Bay Bridge into "the City." *Photo by Fred Matthews*

Shortly after 11 AM on July 16, 1958, Santa Fe Alco PAs lead train No. 13 out of Dearborn Station in Chicago. *Photo by Richard Jay Solomon*

stars, political figures, and business travelers. The streamlined *Super Chief* was an instantaneous success and inspired more streamliners in coming years.

In 1938, a year after *Super Chief,* Santa Fe introduced a host of new streamlined trains. It reequipped its *Chief* as a daily Chicago–L.A. streamliner, while providing a second set of equipment for the *Super Chief* in order to allow that train to provide a twice-weekly service. To appeal to coach passengers, *El Capitan* was added to the Chicago–L.A. run, essentially providing a budget streamliner on roughly the same schedule as the *Super Chief.* For its California clientele, Santa Fe introduced the *San Diegan,* which initially operated twice daily between Los Angeles and San Diego, and the daily *Golden Gate,* a bus and train service connecting Los Angeles and San Francisco. The streamlined train part of the *Golden Gate* operated between Bakersfield and Oakland and the recent completion of the Bay Bridge from San Francisco to Oakland made this service appealing. In order to compete with Southern Pacific and its fancy *Daylights*, Santa Fe's *Golden Gate* offered the lowest fare in the heavily traveled San Francisco–L.A. market. In 1939, Santa Fe supplemented the streamlined *Golden Gate* with a stylized steam-hauled heavy-weight train called the *Valley Flyer*.

Following World War II, Santa Fe made a massive investment in more streamlined trains. It effectively re-equipped the *Super Chief* in the immediate postwar period; then, in 1948 Santa Fe expanded both the *Super*

Santa Fe PA No. 69 leading Train No. 13 at Dearborn Station, Chicago on July 16, 1958. Santa Fe's Alco PAs have long been especially popular with railroad enthusiasts. Four former Santa Fe PAs were bought by Delaware & Hudson and operated by that railroad until the late 1970s when they were sold to Mexico. Recently two were repatriated for restoration. *Photo by Richard Jay Solomon*

Framed by the doorway of the Boiler Shop, a GP20 sits across the transfer table inside the Machine Shop of the Cleburne, Texas, shop complex on September 7, 1988, undergoing a turbocharger overhaul. Born here were the home-made CF7, and SF30C locomotives. At the time of this photo the Cleburne shop was downgraded to a running repair facility with the heavy-class overhauls being split between the shops of Barstow and Topeka. *Photo by Tom Kline*

Chief and *El Capitan* to a daily service. Also in 1948, the new *Texas Chief* initiated streamlined services between Chicago and Texas cities (the train included a Dallas section after Santa Fe's new line to Dallas was completed in 1955). In 1950, the *Kansas City Chief* added a train to the Chicago–Kansas City market. In *Some Classic Trains*, author Arthur D. Dubin asserts that Santa Fe always assigned its best equipment to the *Super Chief* and in 1951 all new equipment was procured for the *Super Chief*, with new cars built by Budd, Pullman, and American Car & Foundry. To the delight of passengers, these new *Super Chief* train sets featured dome cars. One of the greatest pleasures of the streamlined era was riding along in a dome where you could enjoy a panoramic view as the train rolled along. The last of the new streamlined services was the *San Francisco Chief,* introduced in 1954 between Chicago and San Francisco by way of Clovis, where a section from Texas cities to California joined the main train.

Santa Fe introduced a new concept to long distance rail travel in 1956, with the debut of "Hi-Level" streamlined cars on *El Capitan*. Keith L. Bryant indicates that at 15 feet 6 inches tall, these cars were two feet taller than conventional passenger equipment of the period, and designed with greater carrying capacity. Passengers rode on the top level, giving them a better view of the scenery, while the entrance to the cars, baggage, and auxiliary facilities was on the lower level. Santa Fe later ordered additional cars, which were sometimes assigned to its other streamlined trains, such as the *San Francisco Chief*. While Santa Fe's Hi-Level cars remained a novelty in long distance travel for more than two decades, they were the inspiration for Amtrak's Superliner cars, which became the

Santa Fe maintained its passenger trains to a high standard, from Fred Harvey meals sold on its dining cars, to keeping the windows of its trains clean en route. A self-propelled car washer cleans a streamlined Santa Fe passenger car at Albuquerque, New Mexico, in 1968. *Photo by Richard Jay Solomon*

standard long-distance passenger car on western routes in the 1980s.

Branchlines and Mail Trains

Santa Fe's premier long-distance limiteds running from Chicago to the West Coast were by far its best-known, and certainly its best-remembered, service yet by no means its only passenger trains. Santa Fe's branch line networks in Kansas, Oklahoma, Texas, and California played host to numerous passenger locals, trains that played a vital role to the

Santa Fe's *San Diegans* at San Diego display some unusual locomotives in the summer of 1953. On the far left a northbound *San Diegan* is ready to leave for Los Angeles. Santa Fe's lone set of Fairbanks-Morse "Erie Built" cabs with four new coaches are subbing for the regular Budd-built RDC set that often worked this line. On the far right are some of Santa Fe's passenger service EMD FTs. Photographer Fred Matthews notes that this was an unusual lineup for the time and suspects that something was way off schedule. *Photo by Fred Matthews*

communities they served. Traditionally, Santa Fe's branches were served by short passenger trains and mixed trains (combination passenger train and local freight) that typically gathered passengers, mail, and small freight shipments at every stop on a line. These trains would typically operate on daily or triweekly schedules. They were powered by a single, small, steam locomotive hauling just a few cars. Branchlines were the first to be hit by competition from road traffic, and as early as

1909 Santa Fe was looking for ways to reduce the cost of running branch line passenger trains. That year it purchased two "Windsplitter" rail-motorcars from the McKeen Motor Car Company of Omaha, Nebraska. A couple of additional cars followed a few years later. These cars were used to replace steam-powered trains on lightly traveled runs. While the McKeen cars did not prove to be the most reliable technology, Santa Fe liked the concept of self-propelled cars, and in the 1920s

and 1930s, it bought numerous gas-electric cars for branch line services. Popularly known as "Doodlebugs," these cars were usually powerful enough to haul a few cars and might haul an extra coach, baggage, or mail car, and even a boxcar, as traffic demanded.

Santa Fe was one of the busiest rail carriers of the U.S. mail. Many of Santa Fe's named trains carried mail cars, and Railway Post Office cars (RPOs) where mail was sorted en route. RPOs were equipped with specially designed mail hooks that were used for dropping off and picking up mailbags "on the fly" from stations along the way. Santa Fe's premier mail-carrying trains were Nos. 7 and 8, the *Fast Mail Express*, which raced the length of the railroad between Chicago and Los Angeles

by way of the northern route via La Junta, Colorado. This was the only exclusive mail train that ran from Chicago to California over just one railroad and it was among Santa Fe's fastest runs. S. Kip Farrington indicates that in the later steam era, the *Fast Mail Express* was routinely assigned the 84-inch driver 3460 class Hudsons, which would sprint along on level track across Kansas with as many as 16 cars in tow. It was not unusual for this train to hit speeds of more than 100 miles per hour behind steam in the 1930s and early 1940s. In later years, this train was famous for its use of Alco PA diesels, and sometimes as many as eight PA/PBs were used to haul the train over Santa Fe's western lines. At times the *Fast Mail Express* would also carry passenger cars.

Decline to Amtrak

Notwithstanding Santa Fe's gallant efforts to maintain a first-class passenger network by running some of the finest trains on American rails, passenger counts and revenues declined sharply through the 1950s and 1960s. Unlike many American railroads that gradually gave up on their trains as ridership dropped off and allowed services to deteriorate, Santa Fe continued to invest in its trains and maintained them to very high standards. It was buying new passenger equipment as late as 1964, and purchased specialized passenger locomotives (including cowl types) in the late 1960s, at a time when very few railroads were investing in passenger services. Yet, the railroad had no choice but to cut back its services as ridership plummeted.

Branch services were the first to be curtailed, and Santa Fe's branch line trains gradually disappeared from the 1920s onward. Then, as long-distance traffic declined in the face of greater competition from jet planes and

Santa Fe's original transcontinental mainline via Raton and Glorieta retained traditional semaphore signaling through the end of the Santa Fe days into the BNSF era. This was a lightly traveled route in later days hosting only Amtrak's *Southwest Chief* and infrequent freight service. A BNSF military extra led by a former Santa Fe DASH 8-40B approaches Las Vegas, New Mexico, in September 1998. *Photo by Brian Solomon*

Santa Fe was one of the first railroads to negotiate with its labor unions for the discontinuance of cabooses on long-distance freight trains. In the winter of 1983, as this Santa Fe train rolls west though Chillicothe, Illinois, time is running out on the caboose, although few outside the industry were aware of this pending change at the time. *Photo by Steve Smedley*

the construction of the interstate highway system, Santa Fe scaled back its long-distance services. Eliminating service was no simple task and every discontinuance needed approval from the Interstate Commerce Commission, an agency that was often opposed to train cancellation proposals. In 1958, Santa Fe combined its *Super Chief* and *El Capitan* services as a single train, only separating them at times of peak seasonal traffic. In 1965, the *Golden Gate* was discontinued. What doomed the majority of Santa Fe's named trains was the Postal Service's decision to withdraw of most railway post office cars in 1967.

After 1968, Santa Fe only operated a handful of its best-performing trains, including the *Super Chief-El Capitan, San Diegans, San Francisco Chief, Texas Chief,* and *Grand Canyon.*

Viewed from the front porch of the post office in tiny Thompsons, Texas, while the sun sets on a blisteringly hot August 4, 1993, evening, Houston to Newton, Kansas, manifest 524 blares through "town" shortly after starting its journey to the Sunflower State. Hanging over the road and shading the tracks are large magnolias and oak trees that date back to the Civil War. Hauling general non-priority freight daily, train 524 shown here follows the rails of the Galveston Subdivision and will travel straight up the Santa Fe's midsection. *Photo by Tom Kline*

Even this skeletal network was unprofitable and short-lived. In 1971, Santa Fe joined the federally-created Amtrak national passenger network, which assumed operation of most American passenger trains in May of that year. Santa Fe's passenger equipment became a large part of the early Amtrak fleet. In the first years of Amtrak service, its trains over Santa Fe lines looked much the same as they had under Santa Fe operation. In recent years, former Santa Fe routes have hosted several Amtrak trains, including the *Southwest Chief*, and *San Diegans*, trains that display Santa Fe heritage in their names.

Freight Service

The *California Limited*, *Chief*, and *Super Chief* symbolized the romance and prowess of the Santa Fe, but, as with most American railways, it was the line's freight services that generated

Above: In later years, Santa Fe routed most of its freight over its Belen Cutoff over the summit at Mountainair, New Mexico, thus avoiding its original steeply graded lines over Raton and Glorieta Passes. A GE DASH 8-40B leads an eastbound intermodal train through the big curve at Willard, New Mexico, in 1994. *Photo by Brian Solomon*

Next two pages: On October 20, 1979, a Santa Fe train of refrigerated boxcars heavily laden with California produce descends into Mojave, California. Santa Fe operated branches and lines in California's agriculturally rich Central Valley. Fruits and vegetables were transported on expedited schedules to eastern markets. *Photo by Brian Jennison*

Santa Fe was a primary artery for California produce heading east. Using a large fleet of refrigerated boxcars, Santa Fe transported fruits and vegetables to eastern markets. In order to keep produce fresh, the cars carried blocks of ice which were replenished at key points along the line. Produce trains, such as this one seen at Williams, Arizona on July 2, 1955, operated on expedited schedules and were given top priority. Notice the unusual warning signal, which activated when a train was approaching. *Photo by Jim Shaughnessy*

the lion's share of the revenue. In the twentieth century, Santa Fe was a significant freight carrier and its traffic grew enormously in the first decades of the twentieth century as California, Texas, and other regions served by Santa Fe developed and prospered. According to L. L. Waters in his *Steel Trails to Santa Fe*, Santa Fe's freight traffic grew 16-fold in a 50-year period beginning in 1897. Measuring traffic by ton-miles carried, a standard figure, in 1897 Santa Fe carried just over 2 billion ton-miles, while in 1948, it moved nearly 33 billion ton-miles. In 1945, one of the high-water marks of the World War II period, Santa Fe moved approximately 37 billion ton-miles. By the mid-1950s, Santa Fe was one of the largest freight haulers in the United States.

Fruit Trains
California's bountiful agricultural harvest is largely consumed in big eastern states, a fact first made possible by the advent of refrigerated boxcars that allowed consumers to enjoy the fruits of the California harvests

year round. Today, we take for granted fresh oranges and lettuce in the dead of winter, regardless of where we live, but it is important to remember that such luxuries (especially in colder climates) are a function of modern transportation. It was the development of transcontinental railways, like the Santa Fe, that first made it possible to enjoy a fresh salad in New York in January. Santa Fe was among the largest carriers of California produce and it operated a tightly scheduled network of expedited perishable trains known on the railroad as the "Green Fruit Trains," the most famous of which was its GFX. According to S. Kip Far-rington in his book *Railroading from the Rear End*, during 1946 Santa Fe operated more than 14,335 refrigerated boxcars to move more than 100,000 carloads of perishables from California and Arizona, and carried another 25,000 carloads from other states. At that time, the transit time for perishables from California to Chicago was seven days, while California to New York took 10 days.

Traditional refrigerator cars were specially designed insulated boxcars that carried large blocks of ice in them to keep produce from ripening prematurely. Keeping these cars filled with ice required specialized icing facilities at strategic locations along the line. At peak harvest times, Santa Fe would send several long, heavily laden "fruit blocks" eastbound every day. Each of these trains would need to be re-iced about every 24 hours, and re-icing needed to be done as quickly and efficiently as possible. Farrington estimates that in 1945, Santa Fe supplied its trains with more than a million tons of ice. Icing plants were located in Los Angeles, San Bernardino, Calwa, Stockton, Bakersfield, and Needles, California, and along the mainlines at

Winslow, Arizona; Belen and Clovis, New Mexico; La Junta, Colorado; Dodge City and Argentine, Kansas; Fort Madison, Iowa; and Corwith, Illinois. Produce was also collected from farms in Texas, and icing facilities were located at Fort Worth and Cleburne.

Citrus fruit represented about 40 percent of perishable traffic, but a host of other produce was also carried, including broccoli, avocados, and potatoes. Produce trains were loaded at centrally located packing houses, where refrigerator cars were precooled in advance of loading. San Bernardino, east of Los Angeles at the foot of Cajon Pass, was a significant marshalling point for produce traffic. Santa Fe's GFX operated from Los Angeles to Chicago, while the PGX handled perishables from Phoenix to Argentine Yard near Kansas City. In the World War II period, Farrington notes that a loaded refrigerator car weighed about 32 tons. He describes the operation of an eastbound fruit block consisting of 57 loaded cars and 6 empties weighing 3,356 tons.

The advent of mechanized refrigeration resulted in the gradual replacement of traditional insulated cars carrying blocks of ice with modern mechanical refrigerator cars. Perishable traffic declined dramatically as a result of intensive highway competition from the 1950s onward. Santa Fe recaptured some of the perishable business lost to trucks with its progressive intermodal business. Late in the Santa Fe era, some perishable traffic was still carried in refrigerated cars, but by the late 1980s, much of the fruit and vegetable traffic that once rolled along in orange "refers" was being accommodated in mechanically refrigerated truck-trailers, some of which were forwarded by tightly scheduled intermodal trains. The days of the icing docks are long gone.

While transcontinental business provided Santa Fe with lucrative traffic, the railroad also handled local business. In November 1989, Santa Fe 5971 leads the eastbound 938 train, which is meeting the Boron (California) Local at Walong in the Tehachapis. This familiar location is better known as the "Tehachapi Loop." *Photo by Dave Burton*

Bulk Traffic

Santa Fe did not enjoy the level of intensive bulk commodity traffic that benefited some American lines. It was not blessed with vast coal reserves or extensive deposits of iron ore.

However, Santa Fe played a key role in the movement of bulk materials along its lines that contributed to its tide of freight traffic.

Grain movements, particularly Kansas wheat, were among Santa Fe's most notable bulk traffic. The wheat harvest running from roughly July through November kept Santa Fe busy. Traditionally, wheat was moved from a myriad of gathering points on the railroad's branch line network. After the turn of the century, Santa Fe erected an enormous grain elevator at Kansas City for grain storage. For many years, boxcars were the norm for transporting grain, but during World War II enormous strains on equipment availability encouraged Santa Fe to experiment with hoppers for grain shipments. In the modern era, grain was typically moved in unit trains of specially designed covered hoppers weighing 100 tons fully laden. One of the most common paths for grain was from Kansas City to Gulf Coast ports for the export market. A typical modern grain train consisting of roughly 75 cars would be hauled by three to five 3,000 to 3,600 horsepower six-motor diesels.

Mineral traffic had a nominal place on Santa Fe. The railroad had a long history of hauling copper concentrate from mines in Arizona. According to Bryant, after World War II, potash traffic from mines near Carlsbad, New Mexico, developed and in 1969, Santa Fe began hauling bulk trains of molten sulfur from a mine at Rustler Springs, Texas, to Galveston. Coal traffic from York Canyon, New Mexico, south of Raton Pass, developed during the 1960s when Kaiser Steel opened a mine there to supply its steel mill at Fontana, California. From 1966 to 1983, coal trains snaked out of York Canyon on a newly built 37.5-mile branch to reach the mainline at

French, New Mexico, where they would continue to California. Coal was transported in 100-ton hoppers, typically in 84-car trains.

Service ceased when the California steel mill closed. However, in 1992, following changes in air-quality laws that made York Canyon's low-sulfur, high-yield coal more desirable, Santa Fe again began moving unit trains from York Canyon. According to Kevin EuDaly in an article in *CTC Board Railroads Illustrated* magazine, these late-era coal movements typically consisted of 113-car trains that weighed 14,000 tons destined for a Wisconsin Electric plant near Milwaukee. These very heavy trains needed to cross the steeply graded line over Raton Pass. In order to accomplish this they were broken in two sections, which were taken over the mountain one at a time, each requiring six modern General Electric DASH 8-40CW locomotives for the climb, three on the point, and three working as mid-train helpers.

Next two pages: The Tehachapis are best enjoyed on a clear spring morning when the grass is at its greenest, flowers are blooming, and a gentle breeze cools the air. By June, the oppressive summer heat will predominate, the grass will fade to brown, and razor-like thorns will find their way into your socks. On April 3, 1993, a westbound Santa Fe train descending west of Bealville, California, approaches Tunnel 2. *Photo by Brian Solomon*

Below: The allure of the desert is captured in the fading glow of the summer sun. In June 1992, a mixed consist of EMDs climbs west toward Ash Hill near the old station of Trojan in California's Mojave Desert. *Photo by Brian Solomon*

Having slugged out the 16-mile climb west out of the Cimarron River Valley and snaking over the 1 percent Curtis Hill, this Kansas City to Barstow manifest was held and run around by several high-priority intermodal trains. Now it gets back to business and it bears down on the station sign at Tangier, Oklahoma, at 70 miles per hour. The cantilever signal bridge and ubiquitous wooden bridge carrying a country road were Santa Fe trademarks on its busy Chicago to California mainline. *Photo by Tom Kline*

Intermodal Trains

Traditionally, Santa Fe moved its freight in carload trains largely made up of the ubiquitous boxcar. Cars were sorted at yards and terminals all across the system. Among the largest yards were Corwith in Chicago and Argentine near Kansas City, the two gateways where Santa Fe did most of its interchange. Its facilities at Alliance, near Fort Worth, Texas, and Barstow, California, were also very important. In addition, large terminals were operated in Los Angeles and Richmond, California. In the late era, car load traffic took a back seat to intermodal operations. Mike Abalos noted in the November 1995 issue of *Pacific Rail-News* that by the 1980s intermodal trains "outnumbered carload trains by five to one."

In its final form, Santa Fe was epitomized by its high-speed transcontinental intermodal trains, and an in-depth discussion of Santa Fe's intermodal operations could easily warrant a full-length text. Intermodal service, as the name conveys, uses more than one mode. In the railroad context, this initially meant a truck-trailer conveyed on a flatcar. This type of transport offered convenience to the customer, while allowing the railroad to penetrate markets beyond the reach of its tracks. Although not the earliest intermodal carrier, Santa Fe was among the American intermodal pioneers. Beginning in 1952, it introduced an experimental trailer-on-flatcar (TOFC) service between Wichita and Kansas City. Regular intermodal services were initiated in 1954, and by the mid-1950s Santa Fe operated an intermodal network connecting Chicago and Kansas City with terminals in California and Texas.

In *Railroads of the Hour*, published in 1958, S. Kip Farrington indicates that Santa Fe freight No. 39 carried TOFC, and departed Chicago at 6:00 PM and arrived in Kansas City at 7:30 AM the following morning. A Chicago–Los Angeles service was offered in 80 hours, and Chicago–Richmond, California (San Francisco Bay Area), was accomplished in 82 hours. In the early years, these TOFC "Piggy Back" cars were still something of a novelty. It's doubtful that anyone dreamed that Santa Fe's intermodal operations would grow to become the railroad's dominant service.

Although the modern Santa Fe was typified by its high-speed cross-country intermodal trains, the railroad also moved traditional carload traffic. Santa Fe "Shock Control" boxcars are seen rolling eastbound through New Mexico's Abo Canyon. *Photo by Brian Solomon*

During the 1960s, Santa Fe's intermodal business grew rapidly. Its high-speed Chicago to California raceway that had long been a premier passenger route made for an ideal intermodal corridor that allowed the railroad to match over-the-road trucking companies' transit times. Santa Fe pioneered the use of top-lifting cranes in 1963, which reduced the time it took to load and unload truck bodies from flatcars. During 1967, Santa Fe took a leap forward by experimenting with dedicated TOFC trains operated at passenger train speeds. Then, in January 1968, under the direction of Vice President Larry Cena, Santa Fe debuted America's fastest passenger train, the *Super-C*, a high-speed intermodal train connecting Chicago and L.A. on a schedule comparable to Santa Fe's own *Super Chief*. The *Super-C* carried a premium rate and an on-time guarantee. Over the road it was permitted a maximum speed of 79 miles per hour, making it one of

Chillicothe, Illinois was the first crew change west of Chicago. For this crew of a Santa Fe eastbound, it's the end of the run and the end of the day, on March 29, 1983. *Photo by Steve Smedley*

89

Santa Fe moved a lot of intermodal trains. On the evening of February 23, 1995, an eastbound doublestack works east of Winslow, Arizona, near milepost 284. This train carried a number of trailers and containers for J.B. Hunt, a large trucking firm that teamed up with Santa Fe to move transcontinental shipments more efficiently. *Photo by Brian Jennison*

the fastest regularly scheduled freights to ever operate in the United States. Unofficial reports indicate that at times high-rolling engineers pushed that limit in order to keep the train on time (an activity by no means limited to the *Super-C*). As of this writing in 2002, no American railroad operates freight faster than 70 miles per hour, although Santa Fe successor BNSF has contemplated operating an 80 miles per hour service.

The primary customer for the *Super-C* was the United States Postal Service, which by the late 1960s had largely abandoned its once extensive RPO network. In 1976, when the Postal Service shifted its traffic to a Union Pacific routing, Santa Fe was quick to discontinue the extra-fast *Super-C*. By this time Santa Fe had developed a well-established roster of priority intermodal trains. Bryant states that during the 1960s and early 1970s, Santa Fe made a substantial investment in its intermodal business. President John S. Reed, who simultaneously presided over the dismemberment of Santa Fe's passenger network, saw intermodal operations as the way forward. Bryant indicates that in 1968, Santa Fe moved 113,523 TOFC shipments and 1,626 container-on-flatcar (COFC) shipments; just four years later, these numbers had jumped to 156,262 and 22,749, respectively.

When it comes to running freight trains, more horsepower means more speed, and Santa Fe assigned plenty of power to its intermodal trains to ensure they would make it over the road in a timely fashion. Five six-motor units, led by an SD45-2 and a SD45, plus three 3,000 horsepower locomotives, give this eastbound at Bellemont, Arizona, more than 16,000 horsepower with which to get over the road. Barring the unforeseen, it won't be late. *Photo by Don Marson*

In 1974, playing on the fame of its defunct passenger train, Santa Fe introduced a Chicago to L.A. priority-dedicated intermodal train named the *Chief*. In later years, the service was just known as the 188/881 train. A little later, a Chicago to Richmond run known as the *San Francisco Chief* (189/981 train) was inaugurated. Some of Santa Fe's best remembered intermodal runs of the late era were the fast 199/991 trains between Chicago and Richmond that began service in 1975. These tightly scheduled trains that took just 52 hours from terminal to terminal were the domain of the United Parcel Service, and typically warranted Santa Fe's best locomotives.

Although Santa Fe's intermodal loadings grew throughout the 1960s and 1970s, the biggest boost to the railroad's business came with the advent of deregulation during the mid-1970s and culminated with the 1980 Staggers Act, which set the stage for a rejuvenation of the whole railroad transportation industry. The intermodal sector of the market was one of the greatest beneficiaries in the deregulated environment. Staggers gave the railroads the freedom to compete more effec-

Santa Fe's 199 operated on a tight schedule from Chicago to the Bay Area. On a hot summer afternoon in May 1991, a quartet of GP60Ms lead the 199 through Franklin Canyon at Collier, California. Out of sight in an nearby housing development, an ice cream truck plays its compelling tune. In a few weeks, the grass will have bleached from green to gold. *Photo by Brian Solomon*

A silver streak of glint against a foreboding mountain backdrop at 7:17 AM on January 22, 1991, a Santa Fe intermodal train catches the first rays of sun as it approaches Ibis on Goffs Hill in California's Mojave Desert. *Photo by Brian Solomon*

The undulating terrain of northern Arizona sees a never-ending parade of trains over the old Santa Fe. A westbound glints in the setting sun on March 4, 1985 east of Flagstaff. *Photo by Brian Jennison*

tively with other modes by eliminating a host of Byzantine rate regulations that had crippled the industry for decades. Also in the mid-to late-1970s, Santa Fe pioneered new intermodal technology, specifically multi-segment articulated cars designed to reduce the tare weight of intermodal trains, while reducing the amount of slack between the cars, two features designed to reduce costs and improve service.

In the 1980s and 1990s, Santa Fe's intermodal business swelled as its excellent service and new innovations attracted ever more traffic. The advent of the double-stack in the mid-1980s, technology initially shunned by Santa Fe, proved to be a boon, greatly increasing a single train's hauling capacity. During the 1980s, Santa Fe cut its operating costs through improved arrangements with their operating unions that allowed for the elimination of cabooses, trimmed crew sizes, and extended crew districts. Conrail and Santa Fe teamed up in 1987 to run a through coast-to-coast intermodal train, known on Conrail

as TVLA, and on Santa Fe as QNYLA. Twenty years earlier, Santa Fe had discussed a similar operation with Conrail predecessors New York Central/Penn Central, but Central rejected the idea. In 1990, Santa Fe set another precedent when it teamed up with intercity trucking firm J. B. Hunt to haul that company's trailers on Santa Fe's trains.

According to Rich Wallace in the September 1996 issue of *Pacific RailNews*, Santa Fe made a number of concessions to Hunt regarding transit times, load damage and loss, and railroad equipment utilization. The arrangement between railroad and trucking firm proved very satisfactory to both companies, and Santa Fe's business with Hunt boomed. Santa Fe's intermodal business and its finely maintained Chicago to California, Chicago–Texas, and Texas–California corridors were the railroad's most attractive attributes, making it a very desirable merger candidate for both Burlington Northern and Union Pacific. Today, BNSF has continued to develop Santa Fe's intermodal corridors, and business remains robust.

Santa Fe's 500 class DASH 8-40Bs were the preferred intermodal power in the Tehachapis. In the warm glow of the setting sun on March 20, 1994, Santa Fe GEs lug up the grade on the fill between Tunnel 1 and Tunnel 2 east of Caliente, California. *Photo by Brian Solomon*

Right: This August 30, 1986 view of Corwith depicts the yard and control tower. Corwith was Santa Fe's primary Chicago freight yard and the location of an important locomotive shop. *Photo by Mike Danneman*

Bibliography

Books

Bruce, Alfred W. *The Steam Locomotive in America.* New York, 1952.

Bryant, Kieth L. *History of the Atchison, Topeka and Santa Fe Railway.* New York, 1974.

Bush, Donald, J. *The Streamlined Decade.* New York, 1975.

Churella, Albert J. *From Steam to Diesel.* Princeton, N.J., 1998.

Darton, N. H. *United States Geological Survey Bulletin 613: Guidebook of the Western United States, Part C. The Santa Fe Route.* Washington, D.C., 1916.

Drury, George H. *Guide to North American Steam Locomotives.* Waukesha, Wis., 1993.

Drury, George H. *Santa Fe in the Mountains.* Waukesha, Wis., 1995.

Dubin, Arthur D. *Some Classic Trains.* Milwaukee, Wis., 1964.

EuDaly, Kevin. *Santa Fe Rails, Vol. 1.* Kansas City, Mo., 1996.

Farrington, S. Kip, Jr. *Railroading from the Head End.* New York, 1943.

Farrington, S. Kip, Jr. *Railroads at War.* New York, 1944.

Farrington, S. Kip, Jr. *Railroading from the Rear End.* New York, 1946.

Farrington, S. Kip, Jr. *Railroads of Today.* New York, 1949.

Farrington, S. Kip, Jr. *Railroading the Modern Way.* New York, 1951.

Farrington, S. Kip, Jr. *Railroads of the Hour.* New York, 1958.

Glischinski, Steve. *Santa Fe Railway.* Osceola, Wis., 1997.

Marre, Louis A., and Jerry A. Pinkepank. *The Contemporary Diesel Spotter's Guide.* Milwaukee, Wis., 1985.

Marre, Louis A. *Diesel Locomotives: The First 50 Years.* Waukesha, Wis., 1995.

Marre, Louis A., and Paul K. Withers. *The Contemporary Diesel Spotter's Guide, Year 2000 Edition.* Halifax, Pa, 2000.

Marshall, James. *Santa Fe—The Railroad That Built an Empire.* New York, 1945.

McLuhan, T. C. *Dream Tracks: The Railroad and the American Indian 1890–1930.* New York, 1985.

Morgan, David P. *Steam's Finest Hour.* Milwaukee, 1959.

Pope, Dan, and Mark Lynn. *Warbonnets.* Waukesha, Wis., 1994.

Ransome-Wallis, P. *World Railway Locomotives.* New York, 1959.

Reed, S. G. *A History of the Texas Railroads.* Houston, Tex., 1941.

Signor, John R. *Tehachapi.* San Marino, Calif. 1983.

Solomon, Brian. *Trains of the Old West.* New York, 1998.

Solomon, Brian. *The American Diesel Locomotive.* Osceola, Wis., 2000.

Solomon, Brian. *Super Steam Locomotives.* Osceola, Wis., 2000.

Solomon, Brian. *The American Steam Locomotive.* Osceola, Wis., 1998.

Solomon, Brian. *Locomotive.* Osceola, Wis., 2001.

Stover, John, F. *The Routledge Historical Atlas of the American Railroads.* New York, 1999.

Swengel, Frank M. *The American Steam Locomotive, 1: Evolution.* Davenport, Iowa, 1967.

Quiett, Glenn Chesney. *They Built the West.* New York, 1934.

Waters, L. L. *Steel Trails to Santa Fe.* Lawrence, Kan., 1950.

Periodicals

CTC Board Railroads Illustrated, Ferndale, Wash.

Diesel Era, Halifax, Pa.

Pacific RailNews. Waukesha, Wis. (no longer published)

Railroad History, formerly *Railway and Locomotive Historical Society Bulletin.* Boston.

Official Guide to the Railways. New York

Passenger Train Journal. Waukesha, Wis. (no longer published)

TRAINS Magazine. Waukesha, Wis.

Vintage Rails. Waukesha, Wis. (no longer published)

Index

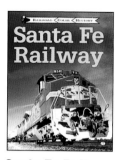

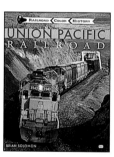

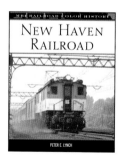